DIANA

UNSEEN ARCHIVES

DIANA

UNSEEN ARCHIVES

ALISON GAUNTLETT

PHOTOGRAPHS BY THE
Daily Mail

p

For Mary and Derek

This is a Parragon Book
This edition published in 2005

Parragon
Queen Street House
4 Queen Street
Bath, BA1 IHE, UK

All photographs © Associated Newspapers Archive
Text © Parragon

Produced by Atlantic Publishing Ltd
Origination by Croxsons PrePress
Design by Judy Linard

A catalogue record for this book is available from the British Library.

ISBN Hardback 1 40544 713 3
ISBN Paperback 1 40544 972 1

Printed in Indonesia

Contents

Introduction

On 29th July 1981, Lady Diana Spencer walked down the aisle to marry Prince Charles in a spectacular ceremony at St Paul's Cathedral. For many years the public had speculated over the woman he would choose as his bride and were entranced when the engagement to Diana was announced. She was the epitome of an English rose with a family background well suited to a future Queen of England. The pomp and splendour were watched by millions of people all over the world and the Archbishop of Canterbury voiced the thoughts of many as he said, 'This is the stuff of which fairy tales are made'.

Diana was born into a family that was very familiar with the traditions of Royalty, her first home being Park House in the grounds of Sandringham. Her maternal grandparents, Lord and Lady Fermoy, had befriended King George VI and Queen Elizabeth (who later became the Queen Mother) and were subsequently offered the lease of Park House, which was passed to Diana's mother, Frances Roche. Diana's father, Viscount Althorp, was appointed equerry to Queen Elizabeth II during which time he and Frances met and subsequently married. Diana was born on 1st July 1961, the third of four children with two older sisters, Sarah and Jane, and a younger brother, Charles.

The early years were overshadowed by their parents' separation and subsequent divorce in 1969, which granted their father custody of the children. Her mother then married Peter Shand Kydd so the youngest two, Diana and Charles, spent most of their time shuttling between the two parents' homes. When she was eight, Diana went to Riddlesworth Hall, a prep school in Norfolk, where she was to be a boarder. Her nanny at this time was Mary Clarke and she remembers her as a girl who loved her food, spending hours outside walking with the dogs, making dens and climbing trees. She was a very talented swimmer and adored the times she spent in the pool on the estate. During these early years Prince Andrew and Prince Edward would often drop by to play in the pool - her first contact with the immediate Royal Family.

In 1973 she followed her sisters to West Heath boarding school in Sevenoaks. She had always wanted to be a ballet dancer but was already five foot nine and had to accept the fact that she was too tall to follow this passion. It was at this school that her talent for communicating with people was first noticed when she was one of the initial volunteers to visit Darenth Park. This was a large hospital for both mentally and physically handicapped people; teachers realised how easily her warmth, laughter and compassion immediately put patients at their ease.

She became Lady Diana in 1975 when her grandfather died and her father assumed the title of Earl Spencer. The family moved to the family seat at Althorp and a year later her father married Raine, daughter of Barbara Cartland. It was on the Althorp estate in November 1977 that Diana first met Prince Charles. She was revising to retake her 'O' levels and he had accepted an invitation to a shoot. Friends recall that Diana had always idolised him and made sure that she was home that weekend!

After failing her retakes she joined the Institut Alpin Videmanette near Gstaad in Switzerland, a traditional finishing school where cookery and skiing took pride of place on the curriculum. However, it was French-speaking and therefore Diana found it difficult to fit in, choosing to leave after a term. Eventually, after pursuing a variety of courses she settled into a flat in the heart of the 'Sloane Ranger' territory and began to work three afternoons a week at a private kindergarten in Pimlico. Despite the fact she had no formal training, Diana was a great success at the school where her natural gift of communication with the children was quickly noticed and soon her hours were increased. In February 1980, she also took on the position of nanny for American businesswoman Mary Robertson, looking after her son Patrick for two afternoons a week.

Charles and Diana met again at various events in 1980 and the relationship began to deepen when she was invited to watch him play polo at Cowdray Park and then to join the party on board *Britannia* for Cowes Week. In September came the invitation to Balmoral for the traditional Royal Family gathering. It gave the young couple the opportunity to spend a great deal of time together and it was during this holiday that the paparazzi first began to suspect a new romance so on her return to London she was immediately shadowed by the media. The famous photograph of Diana in the transparent Liberty skirt was taken at the kindergarten when she was holding one of the children. Soon photographers were camped outside her flat and shots appeared in the newspapers on a daily basis.

In late November and December, the Prince embarked on a tour of India and Nepal and when he returned Diana joined the Royal Family at Sandringham for New Year. Amongst frenzied media speculation, Charles returned from his traditional skiing

trip to Klosters and on 6th February 1981, asked Diana to marry him. She accepted immediately and celebrated that evening with a late-night drive around Buckingham Palace with her three flatmates!

The engagement was officially announced on 24th February 1981 and Diana was moved to Clarence House and then to Buckingham Palace until the day of the wedding. She was soon thrust into official duties of public life and preparations for the wedding began in earnest. Charles was determined to marry at St Paul's Cathedral and very quickly carriages, policemen and soldiers were designated for the procession. The BBC planned to broadcast to seventy-four countries, reaching an audience of 750 million. Diana chose the Emmanuels to make the famous dress but caused them many headaches as she lost two stone and six inches from her waist between the engagement and the wedding.

The marriage took place on 29th July 1981, a perfect summer's day, when hundreds of thousands camped out along the procession route to watch Diana ride past in the Glass Coach, with her father, Earl Spencer. Millions of people around the world watched as she made the three-and-a-half minute walk down the aisle of St Paul's to meet Prince Charles, with her twenty-five-foot train billowing behind her.

After the ceremony, the jubilant crowd cheered them back to Buckingham Palace and they were triumphant when Charles kissed Diana on the balcony of the Palace. Following the wedding breakfast they left by train to travel to Broadlands, the former home of Lord Mountbatten. They spent three quiet days there and then flew to Gibraltar to board the Royal Yacht and sailed around the Mediterranean with 277 sailors for company! The cruise ended in Egypt when they flew to Scotland to spend a month at Balmoral with other members of the Royal Family.

In October they embarked on a short official tour of Wales, their own principality, and it was during the press coverage that she was first given the name 'Diana, the Queen of Hearts'. It was also noticed how pale she had been looking and on 5th November it was announced they were expecting their first child the following summer. Although suffering with debilitating morning sickness throughout her pregnancy, Diana carried out as many official duties as possible. In February, she and Charles holidayed in the Bahamas and as the birth approached she continued to oversee the redecoration of Highgrove, their country home. When in London, they lived

temporarily at Buckingham Palace while their apartment at Kensington Palace was restored and refurbished. They were finally able to move into their apartment in May.

Diana was determined to have their baby at St Mary's Hospital, Paddington. This was revolutionary in immediate Royal circles, as babies had traditionally been born at home. Prince Charles planned to be present throughout the labour and the birth. After a difficult sixteen-hour confinement, Prince William was born on 21st June 1982, the day after the Falklands War ended and two weeks before Diana's twenty-first birthday. The following year, Prince William accompanied his parents on a hugely successful tour of Australia and New Zealand. Wherever they went the crowds clamoured to see Diana and were thrilled with her spontaneity and informality.

Her second pregnancy was announced in February 1984 and Prince Harry was born on 15th September. Both she and Charles were determined that the boys would have as 'normal' an upbringing as possible and although nannies were hired, they both spent as much time with the boys as possible. This also affected their choice of schools later on with the young princes attending kindergartens rather than being educated at home before prep school. They also delayed sending them to boarding schools until they enrolled at Ludgrove.

After Harry's birth Diana gradually resumed her royal duties, accompanying her husband. In 1985, a tour of Italy culminated in a visit to the Vatican for an audience with Pope John Paul II. In October they travelled to Australia and the following month to Washington where at a White House dinner she famously danced with John Travolta before Clint Eastwood cut in! 1986 included a six-day visit to Japan and on a tour of the Arabian Gulf in November Diana was invited to King Fahd's palace – a rare honour for a woman.

By now Diana was fully established in her role as wife to the future king and had gained an international reputation as a fashion icon. Although she found Royal life difficult at times, she was determined to support her husband, be a good mother and carry out the official duties that were expected of her. However, she knew she wanted something more fulfilling and was determined to make a difference to people's lives. In 1987 she realised that the Aids crisis around the world needed help; those suffering from HIV and Aids were stigmatised and many saw it as a self-inflicted disease. The turning point came when she visited the first Aids clinic in England at the Middlesex Hospital and shook hands with a patient. This had an overwhelming impact and the photograph was published all over the world – it now meant that doctors and health workers could start to break down the misconceptions about the disease. She derived a huge amount of satisfaction from this achievement and subsequently embarked on worldwide charity work with Aids sufferers. However, the role that always gave her most pleasure was meeting patients at the clinics where she could sit and talk to them.

In February 1989, her compassion was to help leprosy sufferers in the same way. On an official tour that included Indonesia, she visited a leprosy clinic and sat on the patients' beds holding their hands, again breaking down the social barriers of the disease. She continued to be fully committed to her Royal duties and her own personal charity work, travelling all over the world, often completing gruelling schedules. However, towards the end of the decade and into the early nineties, it was becoming obvious that her marriage was beginning to break down. Photographs were published with Charles and Diana clearly looking unhappy in each other's company and they were spending more and more time apart. In March 1992, her unhappiness was added to by the death of her father, Earl Spencer. She was skiing with her family in Klosters when the news reached her and she immediately flew home. She had always been very close to her father and was clearly distraught at losing him.

Media speculation continued to mount during the year and on 9th December, Prime Minister John Major announced their official separation in the House of Commons. Diana was to live permanently at Kensington Palace while Charles lived at Highgrove. Initially, the role she would play was unclear. She was determined to continue her charity work and now began to organise tours with charities such as the International Red Cross. She also spent as much time with William and Harry as she could, often taking them to everyday places such as Thorpe Park and Disneyland.

On 3rd December 1993, after a very successful year, Diana announced that she would be stepping down from public life. She pleaded with the press that she needed 'time and space' after so many years in the public eye. She did cut down drastically on her public engagements but subsequently resumed more charity work in the following years.

Meanwhile, Prince Charles had been working with reporter Jonathan Dimbleby and his production team, giving them access to his household. An authorised biography and a documentary were planned to celebrate Charles's twenty-fifth anniversary as Prince of Wales. The programme was broadcast on 29th June 1994, to an audience of fourteen million viewers. During the documentary, he admitted to adultery, after their marriage had broken down and at a press conference the next day Camilla Parker Bowles was named. The night this programme was broadcast, Diana made a rare public appearance at a *Vanity Fair* party at London's Serpentine Gallery, looking stunning in the now famous Christina Stambolian dress.

Prince William entered Eton College in September 1995, and the family travelled together for his first day. They all appeared very relaxed and happy together and it was a great day for Diana who always wanted both her boys to board there, to

follow the Spencer family tradition. During the year, reporter Martin Bashir invited her to be interviewed to put across her own interpretation of the events surrounding their marriage. The subsequent programme was broadcast on 20th November 1995 and attracted an audience of twenty-three million viewers. It was during the interview when asked about her future role, she expressed her desire to be 'queen of people's hearts'. In December, Diana flew to New York and received the United Cerebral Palsy Humanitarian of the Year Award from Henry Kissinger. She talked to an audience of fifteen hundred guests about her work as a volunteer; she detailed how fulfilling it was and received a standing ovation.

The divorce was finally made absolute on 28th August 1996. Diana received a lump-sum settlement and was stripped of the title 'Her Royal Highness'. She decided to cut down the majority of her charity work apart from six organisations including the National Aids Trust and the English National Ballet. However, soon after this she became more interested in the anti-landmine campaigns. After speaking to Mike Whitlam of the Red Cross, a working visit was arranged for January 1997. It was decided that they would first travel to Angola where it was estimated there were fifteen million mines scattered in a country that is home to twelve million people. During the visit she toured some of the most devastated parts of the country, saw towns that had been destroyed and visited hospitals that survived with very little equipment and few drugs. Using an interpreter she spoke to patients whose bodies had been torn apart by the mines. Those that travelled with her remarked on the incredible empathy she had for people and how she truly cared for their feelings and the plight they were in. She then famously walked through a half-cleared minefield and publicly detonated a mine

to highlight their devastating effect. In a matter of days the landmine crisis had been brought to the forefront in countries worldwide. In June 1997, she made a significant contribution to major causes after Prince William suggested she sell her dresses at a charity event. After the famous sale the total raised was over three million dollars, the majority going to the Aids Crisis Trust.

In the summer of 1997, Diana and her sons were invited by Mohamed Al Fayed to join his family in St Tropez. The paparazzi soon found them and the three were photographed, obviously having a wonderful time on Fayed's new twenty-million-pound luxury yacht. While she was there, Fayed phoned his son Dodi to join them and he flew down the next day. She returned to London with the boys on 20th July and was instantly inundated with gifts and flowers from Dodi. A brief visit to Paris on 26th July was quickly followed by a few days in London and on 31st July they returned to the South of France to sail around Corsica and Sardinia, obviously enjoying each other's company. Diana then visited Bosnia on 7th August for four days to continue to promote the Red Cross landmine campaign and returned to London on 11th August. She spent some time with her friend Rosa Monckton, cruising around the Greek islands and they returned on 20th August. She had planned to holiday in Milan with another friend, Lana Marks, but this was curtailed when Lana's father died suddenly. Unexpectedly, Diana had a free week and she decided to return to the South of France with Dodi. On 21st August she left England for the last time.

While she was away she phoned many friends and constantly talked of how she was looking forward to seeing William and Harry back in London. They had been with their father at Balmoral and were then going to spend some time with their mother. However, on the morning of 30th August, Dodi told his bodyguards that he planned to take Diana to Paris that day. They visited Dodi's father at his villa that originally belonged to the Duke and Duchess of Windsor and then went on to the Ritz where Diana was to spend the last few hours of her life enjoying a quiet dinner with him. By the time they left the Ritz was besieged by the paparazzi; a plan was formulated so they could try to slip away unnoticed. Dodi and Diana eventually left in a Mercedes driven by Henri Paul, deputy head of security at the Ritz, accompanied by Fayed's bodyguard, Trevor Rees-Jones.

Despite elaborate plans, photographers pursued them and the car followed a dual carriageway that ran alongside the River Seine, to avoid any traffic lights, which might bring them to a halt. In a tunnel which cut underneath the Place de l'Alma, the speeding Mercedes veered to the left and smashed into a pillar killing Dodi and Henri Paul outright. The photographers were the first on the scene and immediately summoned medical help. Diana and Rees-Jones were both alive – Diana was semiconscious but obviously distressed and doctors who were treating her had to wait until she was cut free before she could be transferred to hospital. However, despite the intensive treatment she was given, and as a result of internal injuries, Diana suffered a second major cardiac arrest at the hospital and could not be resuscitated.

She died in the early hours of Sunday 31st August 1997, a month after her thirty-sixth birthday. Information had been relayed to the Royal Family through the night and Prince Charles faced up to the daunting task of waking and telling their two sons of her death. The news was instantly flashed all over the world and the British public, woken by the intense media coverage on the Sunday morning, were stunned as the announcements were made. Prince Charles flew out to escort her body back to England; from Northolt she was taken to the Chapel Royal at St James's Palace. Condolences immediately began to pour in from all over the world and Prime Minister Tony Blair was the first of many to make a public and very emotional tribute to her. The country watched in silence as William and Harry were escorted to Crathie Church for the traditional Sunday service; it was their choice to attend that morning and their faces were tight with emotion.

In the week that followed, people's reaction to her death soon became obvious. At St James's Palace a Book of Condolence was opened and queues soon began to form with people waiting up to twelve hours to sign. Similarly at Kensington Palace, people poured into the grounds to leave flowers, which soon formed a fragrant sea around the house. Her funeral was planned for Saturday 6th September and it was estimated that a million people came to London. Thousands camped in sleeping bags the night before and people waited often twenty deep along the procession route. William and Harry chose to walk behind the coffin and were accompanied by their father, their uncle Earl Spencer and Prince Philip, along the mile long route. The funeral cortège left Kensington Palace with the tenor bell at Westminster Abbey tolling every minute. There was total silence along the route apart from the noise of the horses and the gun carriage on which her coffin lay. As the funeral bearers carried her into the Abbey, television cameras picked out a card on one of the wreaths on the coffin which simply said 'Mummy': it was a last tribute from Harry.

The congregation in the Abbey included guests from all walks of life. Royalty and show business stars sat alongside representatives from charities. The service was carefully planned and included a moving tribute from Elton John who sang a re-written version of 'Candle in the Wind'. Her brother, Earl Spencer, gave a very strong and emotional eulogy and her sisters and the Prime Minister read lessons. At the end of the service the hearse set off towards the family estate at Althorp where she was to be buried. With the family members travelling by train she made this lonely journey with only a police escort for company. People continued to line the route and stand on bridges, waiting for the hearse to pass. Flowers were thrown onto the car and the driver frequently had to stop to clear the windscreen. At Althorp a private family burial was held and Diana's body was laid to rest on an island in the middle of a lake.

Never has the death of someone provoked such a worldwide and lasting reaction. She left a deep impression on those she met when she was alive and her legacy lives on. She brought to the fore issues that needed the public's sympathy and support and was genuine in all the work she did for these causes. Through her charities she met and touched countless people's lives and did what she was determined to do: she 'made a difference'. Her finest legacy is William and Harry: 'her beloved boys'. They were fifteen and twelve when she died and have established a very close bond with their father and each other since her death. Both have matured into good-looking young men with strong beliefs and principles; her influence will always be there. She would be intensely proud of them.

Above: Diana, aged nine, at her mother's house near Itchenor in Sussex. Her parents divorced in 1969 and her mother Frances married Peter Shand Kydd.

A romance begins

The media first realised a growing friendship was
developing between Lady Diana Spencer and
Prince Charles in the autumn of 1980. After she
was invited to holiday with Prince Charles and
the Royal Family at Balmoral, she returned to
London to find photographers camped outside
her flat and the kindergarten where she worked.
Diana was no stranger to the royals, her first
home having been Park House in the grounds of
Sandringham House. Her maternal grandparents
had been great friends of King George VI and
the Queen Mother and childhood playmates
included Prince Andrew and Prince Edward.

Right: The press were waiting outside Diana's
London flat in November 1980. Despite constant
questions, she refused to comment on her
relationship with Prince Charles.

Below: With her eldest sister Sarah, Diana leaves
Princess Margaret's party at the Ritz, in London.

A London address

Images of Diana were captured every time she left her London flat. When she was eighteen, Diana became entitled to a legacy left by her great-grandmother and used it to purchase a flat at 60 Coleherne Court, at the junction of Old Brompton Road and Redcliffe Gardens. Close friends then rented rooms from her. She mixed with the wealthy young set that lived around Sloane Square, dubbed 'Sloane Rangers' by the media. Weekends were usually spent in the country and she went skiing every year.

After a brief spell at finishing school in Switzerland, she had pursued a variety of courses and jobs, but eventually found employment three afternoons a week in the Young England kindergarten, at St. Saviour's Hall, Pimlico. Fees were £200 a term and the children were generally from very wealthy families. Diana was an instant success at the kindergarten, popular with staff, parents and children alike. Despite the absence of any formal training, she demonstrated a natural gift for communicating with children and was highly praised by the principal, Kay Seth-Smith.

Kindergarten days

As she supervised the children from the kindergarten playing in St. George's Square, the famous shot was taken of "Shy Di" wearing a Liberty skirt that became transparent in the sunshine. Apparently, Prince Charles on seeing the photograph remarked, 'I knew your legs were good but I didn't realise they were that spectacular. And did you really have to show them to everybody?'

Nanny Diana

After working at the kindergarten for a time, she also took on the position as nanny to American businesswoman Mary Robertson, looking after her son Patrick for two afternoons a week. The public continued to speculate about Diana and Prince Charles who, at the time, were meeting at secret locations including friends' houses.

1981

The Engagement

A royal engagement

The engagement was officially announced at 11am on 24th February, and Lady Diana and Prince Charles posed happily in the grounds of Buckingham Palace.

He had proposed to her on 6th February, at the Palace, after a private supper and she accepted immediately. The engagement ring, supplied by Garrard's, the royal jewellers, was a large oval sapphire surrounded by fourteen diamonds and set in eighteen-carat white gold, and cost a princely £28,500. The Royal Family gave her a diamond and emerald pendant depicting the emblem of the Prince of Wales, which had previously belonged to Queen Mary.

First official function

Diana was immediately moved to
Clarence House and then to Buckingham
Palace, until the day of the wedding. It was
soon time for her to attend her first official
function and in March she accompanied
Prince Charles to a recital in Goldsmiths Hall
(*opposite*). She wore a revealing strapless silk
taffeta gown and, on arrival, Prince Charles
proudly told waiting photographers, 'You
won't believe what's coming next' as she
stepped out of the car.

Right: Later that month Diana travelled to
Sandown to watch Prince Charles ride in the
Horse and Hound Grand Military Gold Cup.
He was unseated a mile from the finish but
fortunately came away relatively unscathed.

Below: Diana at Sandown with Charles's
friend, Andrew Parker Bowles.

Visit to Tetbury

In May, Diana and Prince Charles made an official visit to Tetbury in Gloucestershire to open a new operating theatre at the local hospital. After their marriage, the royal couple would live nearby at Highgrove, a nine-bedroomed Georgian house built in 1796 for John Paul Paul. The Duchy of Cornwall had purchased it in 1980 as a private country residence for the Prince of Wales. During the months leading up to the wedding, Diana oversaw the refurbishment of the house while Charles focused on the gardens and surrounding land. The people of Tetbury presented them with two large ornamental gates as a wedding present so they would have greater security and privacy.

Wedding preparations

Opposite above: On 11th June, Charles and Diana visited St Paul's Cathedral. Charles had specifically requested that they be married at the Cathedral where he preferred the acoustics and architecture to those of the more traditional Westminster Abbey. The organisation of the wedding was in the hands of the Lord Chamberlain and was to be on a mammoth scale. Eleven carriages would be used, with three thousand policemen and three thousand soldiers lining the route. Television companies planned the largest-ever outside broadcasting event.

Opposite below: During a visit to Cheltenham Police Headquarters, where the force responsible for Highgrove's security was based, eighteen-year-old-schoolboy Nicholas Hardy kissed Diana's hand.

Right: A quiet moment during a polo match for the bride-to-be, a month before her wedding.

Polo-playing Prince

Prince Charles is a very committed
polo player and Diana often
accompanied him to matches. The
weekend prior to their wedding, he
played in a match at Guards Polo Club,
organised by Major Ronald Ferguson
(who also managed Charles's polo
team). Diana spent much of the time
talking excitedly to his daughter Sarah,
already a good friend.

One of the best-kept secrets before the
wedding was the design of Diana's
dress. To make it, she had selected the
Emmanuels, who had created the black
taffeta evening dress for her first public
engagement. Her final choice was a
fairy-tale confection made with forty-
five feet of ivory silk taffeta.

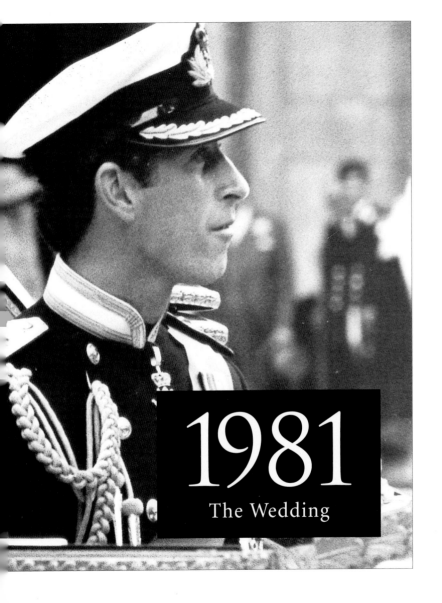

1981

The Wedding

The marriage service

Prince Charles and the twenty-year-old Lady Diana Spencer were married on 29th July 1981, a perfect summer's day. Prince Charles rode with his supporter, Prince Andrew, in an open carriage, while Diana shared the famous Glass Coach with her father, Earl Spencer. As she emerged from the coach at the steps to the Cathedral, the waiting public were finally able to see the stunning dress with its twenty-five-foot train. It had been made by one seamstress, Mrs Nina Missetzis, working in a locked room, and had ten thousand pearls and mother-of-pearl sequins hand-sewn onto the bodice. Together, Diana and her father made the three-and-a-half-minute walk down the aisle, accompanied by Jeremiah Clarke's *Trumpet Voluntary*. Her father was very shaky after a recent stroke, but was determined to give her away. Charles and Diana were married by the Archbishop of Canterbury, Dr. Robert Runcie, who pronounced, 'This is the stuff of which fairy tales are made.'

Newlyweds

The service was relayed outside, and the moment after their vows were made, jubilant applause could be heard echoing through the surrounding streets. In their nervousness, Diana had muddled Charles's names and he had agreed to share her worldly goods but not his own. Diana's wedding ring was made from a nugget of Welsh gold mined in 1923 and previously used for the wedding rings belonging to the Queen Mother, the Queen, Princess Margaret and Princess Anne. At the end of the service, the newly married couple emerged from the west door of St Paul's to be greeted by cheering crowds.

The procession route

An estimated million people lined the procession route back to Buckingham Palace, while approximately 750 million watched around the world. Thousands had camped out in the streets overnight, revelling in the spirit of the all-night party. As Charles and Diana rode through the streets in their open carriage, the crowds roared in delight.

The balcony at Buckingham Palace

As the procession finished, barriers were moved and well-wishers poured down the Mall to surround Buckingham Palace. Just after one o'clock the doors to the balcony opened and Charles and Diana stepped out, to be greeted by a huge and appreciative crowd. The atmosphere was electric and the cheering grew louder and louder; finally, in response to persuasive chants, Charles kissed his bride. After the wedding breakfast, the couple left for Waterloo Station in a carriage festooned with twenty silver heart-shaped balloons and a gaudily decorated 'Just Married' sign, courtesy of Princes Andrew and Edward.

Honeymooners

From Waterloo, Charles and Diana travelled to Broadlands, home of the late Lord Mountbatten. They spent three lazy, secluded days here and then Prince Charles piloted an RAF Andover of the Queen's Flight to Gibraltar, where they were to board the Royal Yacht *Britannia*. For two weeks, the couple sailed around the Mediterranean, accompanied by a crew of 277, plus the band of the Royal Marines. After the cruise, they flew to Lossiemouth in Scotland to spend a month at Balmoral, along with other members of the Royal Family, there for the traditional summer break.

Left and opposite above: At Balmoral, the newlyweds strolled along the banks of the River Dee, deeply suntanned and holding hands. When asked about married life they both said coyly they could 'highly recommend it'. At the end of October, the Prince and Princess of Wales embarked on an official three-day tour of Wales, their own principality. It was on this tour that Diana's immense popularity with the public was first noticed. Wherever they went, the waiting crowds were desperate to see her and were entranced by her informality. Traditional royal handshakes were not her style – she wanted to reach out spontaneously to touch people and cuddle children. She was an instant hit.

Opposite below: Diana meets some of the waiting crowds at Haverfordwest.

Mum-to-be

Some people had noticed how pale Diana had been looking during the Welsh tour and on 5th November her pregnancy was announced, with their first baby due the following summer. From early on in the pregnancy, she suffered from very debilitating morning sickness and as a result, many public engagements had to be cancelled.

Above and left: Diana's arrival at the Royal Opera House to watch a performance of the ballet *Romeo and Juliet.*

Opposite right: Girlish and demure, Diana attended a function at the National Film Theatre with Prince Charles to celebrate the twenty-fifth anniversary of the London Film Festival.

Opposite far right: A solo engagement in November when Diana switched on the Regent Street Christmas lights.

Remembrance Day at the Cenotaph

Above: Diana stands on the balcony overlooking the Cenotaph with King Olaf of Norway and Princess Alice.
Opposite: In Tetbury, near to Highgrove, Diana was snapped dashing from her car into a local newsagent's to buy a magazine. She soon realised that she would always be in the public eye, regardless of whether she was attending an official function or going about her daily life.

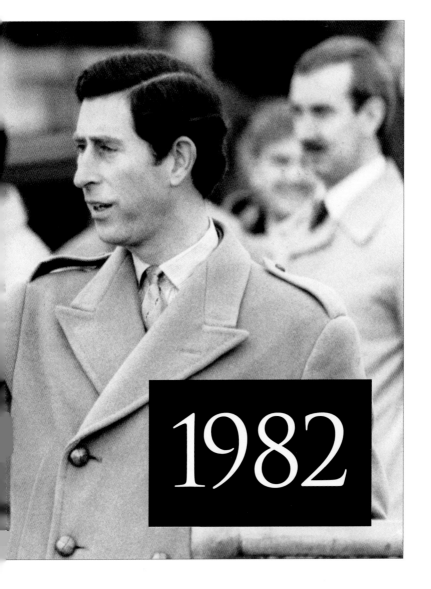

1982

Planning the birth

From a very early stage in the pregnancy,
Charles and Diana had decided that rather
than follow royal tradition and have their
baby at one of the official royal residences,
she would give birth in the private Lindo
Wing at St. Mary's Hospital, Paddington.
Diana was a firm believer in natural
childbirth and exercised regularly, taking
breathing and relaxation lessons from a
very experienced midwife, in readiness for
the labour.

Opposite: As the pregnancy advanced
Diana resumed royal duties and in January
she accompanied Charles on a visit to the
Dick Sheppard School in Tulse Hill.

Left and above: The royal couple arrive at
Westminster Abbey for the Royal College
of Music Centenary Service.

Kensington Palace

For the first ten months of married life, Charles and Diana's London base was a flat in Buckingham Palace, while an apartment in Kensington Place was restored and refurbished for them. They were finally able to move there in May, only weeks before their baby was due.

Opposite: After attending the charity performance of *Little Foxes* at the Victoria Palace Theatre, Diana met Elizabeth Taylor backstage.

Right: On a visit to open the Albany Community Centre in Deptford, South East London, Diana was told by a mother of five-year-old twins that, however many books you read about children, you don't actually learn until you have them.

Below: Three weeks before her due date, Diana was at Smith's Lawn to see Prince Charles play polo.

Welcome Prince William

Opposite: Prince William was born at 9.03pm on
21st June, weighing 7lb 1oz. As planned, he was
born at St. Mary's, with Prince Charles present
throughout the birth. It had been a long, sixteen-
hour labour and when Prince Charles emerged
from the hospital at 11pm that night he confessed,
'I'm overwhelmed by it. It was a very grown-up
experience'. The Queen ordered a forty-one gun
salute both in Hyde Park and at the Tower of
London. Diana decided to leave the hospital at
6pm the following evening, smiling happily to the
waiting crowds. Ten days later, on 1st July, she
would celebrate her twenty-first birthday.
Above and right: On 26th July, Diana attended
her first public engagement after William's birth:
the Falkland Islands Thanksgiving Service at St
Paul's Cathedral. William had been born the day
after the war ended.

William Arthur Philip Louis

Opposite: William was christened on 4th August in the Music Room at Buckingham Palace. This date was chosen to coincide with the Queen Mother's eighty-second birthday. The Archbishop of Canterbury, Dr. Robert Runcie, led the baptismal service and the long list of godparents included former King Constantine of Greece; Lady Susan Hussey, one of the Queen's senior Ladies-in-Waiting; Princess Alexandra; Lord Romsey, Lord Mountbatten's grandson; Sir Laurens van der Post, and the Duchess of Westminster. Following royal custom, William wore a robe of Honiton lace, first used for Victoria and Albert's babies, and was baptised with water from the River Jordan, a tradition that reaches back to the Crusades.

Right: Diana attended the wedding of former flatmate Carolyn Pride to William Bartholomew.

Below: After opening an extension to the Royal School for the Blind in Leatherhead, Surrey, Diana stopped to talk to the children who came to greet her.

Evening engagements

Opposite: Diana attending a charity dinner and fashion show at the Guildhall in London. After the birth of Prince William she had suffered postnatal depression and lost a significant amount of weight. She slowly regained her health and a year later was pregnant once more.
Above: Diana was welcomed at a concert at the Whitbread Brewery in London.

Representing the Royal Family

The Royal Family were at Balmoral when they learnt of the death of Princess Grace of Monaco in a car accident. Diana had previously met her on her first public engagement. She had been very nervous and Princess Grace had taken the time to reassure her and give her confidence – an act that Diana had always remembered. Diana was keen to attend the funeral and the Queen allowed her to represent the Royal Family on her own.

Above: In November, Queen Beatrix and Prince Claus of the Netherlands made a state visit to Britain. They were welcomed at Westminster Pier by several members of the Royal Family including the Prince and Princess of Wales. A two-day tour of Wales was scheduled for the royal couple the same month and the visits included Aberdovey *(left)* and Wrexham *(opposite)*.

A hardworking royal

Above: A visit to the wreck of the *Mary Rose* in Portsmouth. Although Diana did not always find it easy to adapt to protocol, she began to settle into life as a member of the Royal Family.
Opposite: Accompanying Prince Charles to the premiere of the film *Gandhi*. The presence of the Princess ensured that the photographers and fashion writers turned out in force.

Health visits

Left: On a visit to the Department of Health and Social Security, Diana was greeted by MP Norman Fowler and staff on a twenty-four-hour strike over alleged under-manning of offices. The strikers, however, deemed her visit to be charity work and allowed her through their picket line.

Below: Just prior to Christmas, Diana visited the Royal Marsden Hospital in Fulham, where she spent an hour meeting staff and chatting to cancer patients.

Opposite: At the Charlie Chaplin playground for handicapped children in Kennington Park, London, Diana confessed to wearing Damart thermal underwear for her outdoor winter functions.

1983

Walkabouts

The year began with Charles and Diana taking their first skiing holiday together in Lech, Austria. At times, Diana found it difficult to cope with the persistent paparazzi who followed her wherever she went. At home, William was now six months old. Diana adored him: nanny Barbara Barnes cared for him but Diana spent as much time with him as she could. She missed her son terribly on the Austrian holiday and vowed from that moment to avoid any unnecessary separations. His parents soon found themselves abbreviating his name to Wills.

Opposite: In February, Diana visited Nightingale Home for the Elderly in South West London.

Above: A fifteen-thousand-strong crowd came to see Diana open the new £7 million shopping centre in Aylesbury, Buckinghamshire. She took the opportunity to talk and joke with them afterwards.

Left: Meeting the crowds in Tavistock, Devon.

And baby came too

In March, Charles and Diana embarked on a six-week tour of Australia and New Zealand and at Diana's insistence William came with them. She knew that Charles had endured months of separation from his parents and neither of them was prepared to leave William for this long. Nanny Barbara Barnes accompanied them and looked after William at a base in New South Wales, while his parents flew across the continent, completing a gruelling schedule. Charles and Diana saw their son in between official engagements, and to mark the occasion William crawled for the first time. Diana was an instant hit with the Australians, who came out in their thousands to see her, and as Charles guided her through the protocol of official life, her confidence began to grow.

Left: At a charity ball in Sydney, Charles whisked Diana around the dance floor as she pleaded with him to slow down – they were clearly enjoying themselves.

Below: Charles and Diana attended a luncheon at the Dorchester Hotel in aid of the Leukaemia Research Fund and the Injured National Hunt Jockeys Fund.

Above: Back in England, Diana visited a playground for handicapped children in Cheltenham. The children's delight at meeting her was matched by her obvious pleasure in their company.

Summer visits

Left: The Prince and Princess of Wales in fancy dress at Fort Edmonton, Canada. They had attended a costume barbecue where guests dressed in styles from the Gold Rush age. Diana's dress - earlier worn by actress Francesca Annis when she played Lillie Langtry in a TV drama series - was very heavily boned and apparently quite a relief to take off at the end of the evening.

Opposite: At the premiere of the new Bond film *Octopussy* Diana, who appeared to have lost yet more weight, met the movie's producer, Cubby Broccoli.

Honouring the Spencer family

Top: In July, Diana opened the new Admissions Unit of St Andrew's Hospital in Northampton. The building was named Spencer House, in honour of the Spencer family's long service to the hospital. She attended the ceremony with her father and stepmother, Lord and Lady Spencer. ***Above:*** Prince Charles and Diana together at Stoke Mandeville Hospital with Jimmy Savile. ***Opposite:*** The Variety Club Sunshine Coach luncheon was held at the Guildhall in July, with Diana as guest of honour.

Noel Coward's
Hay Fever

Left and opposite: The Queen's Theatre, Shaftesbury Avenue was the venue for a charity performance of Noel Coward's *Hay Fever*. Diana arrived wearing an exquisite silk evening gown that drew gasps from the waiting crowds.

Below: After the performance, Diana was introduced to actress Penelope Keith. By now, features on Diana's clothes and style were regularly appearing in newspapers and magazines. She had brought glamour to the Royal Family and her clothes and hairstyles were assiduously copied. She chose British designers to support and promote the country's fashion industry.

Proud parents

Opposite below: William at eighteen months, in the gardens at Kensington Palace. He showed a natural curiosity for the world and had already established a reputation for being a mischievous toddler, earning the nickname of Wombat.

Above: Despite the rain, Diana met the waiting crowds outside the Asian Centre in Walthamstow in November.

Opposite above: Children at the West Indian Family Centre in Brixton chatted and sang to Diana. They were delighted when she broke into an impromptu calypso dance.

1984

Expecting again

Diana's second pregnancy was announced on St. Valentine's Day, with the next baby due in September. Diana later revealed that she and Charles had a very close relationship in the months before Harry's birth.

Opposite: The Royal Marsden Hospital in Sutton welcomed her on a cold February morning.

Above left: At a Jewish Welfare Board dinner held at the Guildhall, Diana was presented with flowers and a tiny rocking chair for the new baby.

Above right and right: As she visited the knitting factory of T W Kempton Ltd in Leicester, employees showed her some of the baby clothes they made.

Smiling through

During her second pregnancy Diana again suffered from morning sickness, which often lasted throughout the day.

As she opened a £2 million spinal injuries unit at the Royal National Orthopaedic Hospital in Stanmore, she looked very queasy at times. However, she continued to laugh and joke with patients and the waiting crowds.

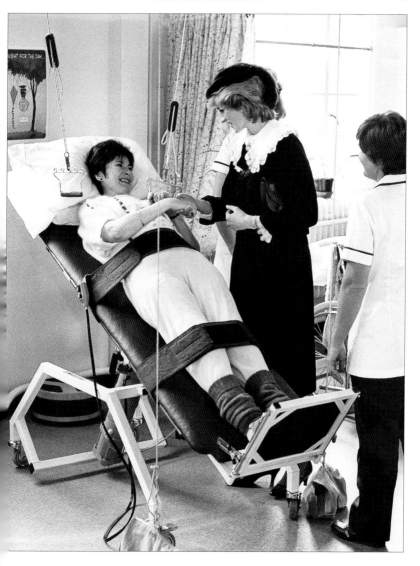

A very popular Princess

Above: After a tour of the Royal Doulton factory in Burslem, Stoke-on-Trent, Diana received many good wishes from the crowds. In contrast to her first pregnancy, when she wore over-sized maternity clothes, Diana presented a much more slimline shape the second time around. She put on less weight and wore clothes that concealed rather than accentuated her pregnancy. She was again planning to have the baby at St. Mary's in Paddington.

Right and opposite: The pearly King and Princess of Deptford in South East London greeted her as she visited the Albany Centre in the town.

Gifts for William and the new baby

Above: A crowd of ten thousand gathered to watch the Prince and Princess of Wales unveil a memorial to Lewis Carroll in the middle of Warrington. The fourteen-year-old son of the licensee of the Mad Hatter pub presented her with two specially bound editions of *Alice in Wonderland* for Prince William and the new baby.

Opposite: On a walkabout in Glastonbury.

Right: After officially opening Callard and Bowser's new £8 million sweet factory near Bridgend, Diana then toured the plant.

Charles and Diana at the movies

Right and below: At the charity premiere of *Indiana Jones and the Temple of Doom* Diana and Charles greeted members of the film's cast after the screening.

Opposite above: Although Diana preferred pop music to opera, the couple had the opportunity to meet tenor Luciano Pavarotti, who became one of her favourite performers.

Opposite below: In July, Diana attended the Royal Tournament at Earls Court with Prince Charles.

Last engagements before the birth

Opposite: Diana was a keen spectator at Cirencester when she watched Charles's polo
team win 7-6.
Above: A visit to King's College Hospital in the last few weeks before her second baby was due.

Prince Harry is born

Left: Four weeks before the birth and two weeks before her twenty-third birthday, Diana had flown to Scotland to join the Royal Family at Balmoral. Her uncle Lord Fermoy had just died and she was visibly upset. Prince Henry Charles Albert David was born on Saturday 15th September weighing 6lb 14oz. Diana had gone into labour that morning while at Windsor and was immediately driven to the hospital, with a police escort. The following day, Prince Charles brought William to see his new brother, who would soon be known as Harry.
Below: Members of the public and the media waited outside St. Mary's all day to hear news of the impending birth.
Opposite: Diana left the hospital with the newborn prince on Sunday 16th September to return to Kensington Palace.

Back in the public eye

Opposite and above left: Diana resumed her
public engagements soon after Harry's birth
and in November visited the Dr Barnardo
Centre in Newham, East London. She met
staff and children to find out more about the
various activities in which they were involved.
Above right: A visit to the Children's Centre,
Ealing, in November.
Right: Diana was surrounded by crowds
as she arrived to launch the P&O liner
Princess Royal.
In December, Prince Harry was christened
Henry Charles Albert David at St. George's
Chapel, Windsor. His godparents were Lady
Celia Vestey, Lady Sarah Armstrong Jones,
Carolyn Bartholomew (Diana's former
flatmate), Prince Andrew, Bryan Organ (royal
artist) and Gerald Ward.

An audience with Dame Edna!

Above: Greeting Dame Edna Everage (Barry Humphries).
Opposite above: With a senior youth worker at the Victoria Centre in Wellingborough.
Opposite below: Lady Wolfson presented Diana with two small pairs of roller skates at a charity performance of *Starlight Express* at the Apollo Theatre.

1985

President of Dr Barnardo's

Above and opposite below: Princess Diana was President of Dr Barnardo's and in February made a visit to their headquarters in Tanners Lane, Ilford. She took a great interest in the work of the charity and was very moved by the plight of some of the children. As she left, she was cheered by the youngsters awaiting fostering or adoption in the Barnardo's Village next door. *Opposite above:* A very enthusiastic greeting from members of the Broadwater Farm Youth Association.

Determined to get there despite the snow

Opposite: The Princess had made a personal request to visit the foundation for the study of infant deaths at Peterhouse College, Cambridge, and was not deterred by the several inches of snow that fell on the day scheduled for her visit. She told one of the founder members, 'I'm a mother – that's why I couldn't get here fast enough.'

A Home Office pathologist had recently claimed that most cot death victims were smothered by mothers or fathers, causing immense distress to bereaved parents. Diana was determined to give her support, and bereaved parents were very touched by her visit and sympathetic words.

Right: Diana takes time out from royal duties to attend the private wedding of a friend.

Supporting the Prince of Wales Trust

Opposite: When Phil Collins gave a concert in aid of the Prince of Wales Trust, he met Diana afterwards and gave her two tiny tour jackets for William and Harry.

Below: The Prince and Princess of Wales visited the King's Troop Royal Horse Artillery in St. John's Wood, London. In April, Charles and Diana were on an official tour of Italy that began in Sardinia. During an audience with Pope John Paul II, Diana ensured she was appropriately dressed in an ankle-length black dress and black lace mantilla. William and Harry were flown out to join their parents when they reached Venice, so they could all enjoy a short Mediterranean cruise, aboard *Britannia.*

Left: A smiling Diana on a visit to Cirencester Police Station.

Continuing the work for Barnardo's

Above right: In March, Diana carried out her first public engagement for Dr Barnardo's, now renamed simply Barnardo's, when she attended a fashion gala in London. She wore a sensational silver pleated dress designed by Bruce Oldfield, a former Barnardo's boy, who organised the event.
Opposite: Princess Anne joined Diana and Charles for the film premiere of *A Passage to India*.
Above left: An opportunity for Diana again to meet Dame Kiri Te Kanawa, at a gala concert in aid of the Westminster Children's Hospital, at the Banqueting Hall, Whitehall. Dame Kiri had sung Handel's *Let the Bright Seraphim* at Diana's marriage to Prince Charles four years previously.
Right: Diana adopts a nautical look for a visit to the Isle of Wight in May.

Dropping in for a chat!

Left: Diana says farewell to a resident after stopping for a chat through his window, during a visit to the Poolmead Centre of the Royal National Institute for the Deaf in Bath.

Opposite above left: At times, critics claimed that she was too extravagant with her wardrobe but this Bruce Oldfield dress had another outing for the premiere of A *View to a Kill* at the Odeon, Leicester Square.

Opposite above right and below: Unperturbed by the rain, a smiling Diana met crowds at the Ravenswood Foundation at Crowthorne in Buckinghamshire, a centre for the care of people with learning difficulties.

Live Aid

Above: In July, Diana opened a new wing at Lincoln County Hospital. That same month, the Prince and Princess attended the Live Aid concert, a concept dreamed up by pop singer Bob Geldof. The sixteen-hour event was held simultaneously at Wembley Stadium and JFK Stadium in Philadelphia, to raise money for the starving in Ethiopia. The concert was seen by 1.5 billion people and eventually raised $40 million through donations and phone pledges. Diana was seen bopping along to the music, fully behind the initiative.

Opposite above: Princess Diana and Prince Andrew attended the marriage of the Hon. Carolyn Herbert to John Warren. The wedding was held at Highclere Castle in Berkshire.

Opposite below: A delighted princess watched her husband's polo team beat Brazil 6-5 in the Silver Jubilee Cup. Charles was playing for the England II polo team at the Guards Polo Club in Windsor.

Stoke Mandeville

Opposite: Diana opened The International Stoke Mandeville Games at the end of July.
Above: On a visit to the Remploy factory in Coventry, where she was presented with a leather attaché case.

Her 'beloved boys'

Opposite and right: The family boarded the Royal Yacht *Britannia* in August, to join other members of the royal party as they cruised around the Western Isles. At the end of the holiday they would all travel to Scotland for the traditional stay at Balmoral, until October.

Below: At the age of three it was time for William to make the transition into childhood. Traditionally, children in the Royal Family had been educated at home at this early age, but Diana wanted William to mix with his peers and make his own friends, so his parents eventually chose Miss Mynors' kindergarten in London's Notting Hill Gate. After much preparation, including the installation of additional security, William arrived for his first day at school in September. It was a very happy school with three classes, each with twelve children.

Solo visits

Right and below: On a solo visit to a military base in West Berlin in the autumn it was clear that Diana was gradually carrying out more engagements on her own.
Opposite above and below: During a visit to St. Joseph's Hospice in Hackney, East London, Diana took the opportunity to joke with patients.
In October, Sir Alastair Burnet interviewed the Prince and Princess of Wales. Twenty million viewers watched the programme as they talked frankly and happily about their lives together.

Tour of Australia and the USA

Above: The royal couple took the opportunity to kiss when the cup was awarded after a polo match, at Werribee Park in Australia.

Opposite and right: Diana again set the fashion trends when she attended the races in Australia on Melbourne Cup Day. When the tour reached the USA the Prince and Princess attended a White House dinner in Washington where Diana danced with both *Saturday Night Fever* star John Travolta and actor Clint Eastwood. Prince Charles, meanwhile, was waltzing with the First Lady, Nancy Reagan.

Criticism from the Australian fashion experts

Opposite: Despite being celebrated as a fashion icon around the world for her fabulous sense of style, she had to endure criticism from Australian fashion writers, who claimed that this outfit was dowdy and that she had saved her best for the States.

Above: On their return from the tour, the Prince and Princess attended the Birthday Ball at the Albert Hall in aid of the Birthright charity. Her brother Charles, Viscount Althorp, greeted her.

Uptown Girl

Left and below: Wearing a stunning, backless, crushed velvet evening gown, Diana met Stephen Spielberg after the premiere of his film *Back to the Future,* at the Empire Theatre.
Opposite: A fabulous shot of the Princess as she arrived at the Odeon, Leicester Square for the premiere of *Santa Claus.*
Diana had secretly been working with dancer Wayne Sleep to surprise her husband. Charles was due at a Royal Gala performance at Covent Garden and she wanted to appear on stage performing a dance for him. After numerous clandestine rehearsals at Kensington Palace, the Prince and Princess attended the performance. Just before the end she appeared, dancing to Billy Joel's 'Uptown Girl'. Charles was speechless and she received eight curtain calls from a delighted audience!

Meeting the children

Opposite above: On a visit to the Bentham Estate Tenants Association in Islington, she turned down the offer of a sweet from one of the four-year-olds. She had been touring the pre-school playgroup and the Bean Club for Youth.

Above: While visiting the Bentham Estate, Diana met the Senior Supervisor of the child playgroup and was clearly in an environment she loved.

Opposite below: Leaving Sandringham Church with Prince Andrew, Princess Anne and her daughter, Zara Phillips during the Christmas celebrations.

1986

Working with deaf people

Below: At a visit to the Deaf Centre in Northampton, Diana was put through her paces on the snooker table. Much to the fifteen-year-old's delight, Diana potted a red straight away. Afterwards she was able to answer several silent questions from the children as she put her lip-reading skills to the test. Most wanted to ask her about Princes William and Harry.

Opposite below: When Diana visited the West Midlands, members of the Litchfield Deaf Church performed the hymn *God Be in my Head* using sign language. The Chaplain for the Deaf, Father George Moody, greeted her.

Opposite above: On a visit to Ridgway House Retirement Home for the Elderly in Towcester, Diana stopped to talk to some schoolchildren.

Left: In her role as President of the Royal Academy of Music, Diana attended a choral concert at the Royal Academy in Marylebone Road, London.

Always at ease with children

Above and opposite: Meeting children and
well-wishers at the Markfield project, North
London.
Left: Diana arrives at the Empire Theatre,
Leicester Square.
During the previous year, Diana had played
cupid as a romance between Prince Andrew
and Sarah Ferguson began to develop. Diana
and Sarah had always been close friends,
lunching together regularly. After Sarah was
invited to Windsor for Royal Ascot, Prince
Andrew asked her to join him at Balmoral for
the summer break. She accompanied Charles
and Diana for a skiing holiday in Klosters and
for once media attention was away from
Diana as the paparazzi rushed to photograph
Sarah Ferguson. Prince Andrew proposed to
her later that month.

Gardening accident

Above: When Diana and Charles arrived at St. George's Chapel, Windsor, Charles was wearing a sling having accidentally hit a finger while hammering in a stake in the garden.

Opposite: With other representatives of the Royal Family, Charles and Diana met the President of the Federal Republic of Germany and Freifrau von Weizsacker who were in Britain for a four-day state visit. Their arrival at Victoria Station was followed by a carriage procession to Buckingham Palace.

In May, Charles and Diana travelled to Japan for a six-day tour. There was much excitement in Japan, where more people than in Britain had watched the royal wedding. The dress Diana wore on arrival was printed with the symbol of the rising sun. It was a very heavy schedule, with twenty-nine engagements, and they were often working for twelve hours a day. In Kyoto, after watching a traditional tea ceremony, Diana was presented with a kimono. The Japanese dressmakers had overestimated her height and she nearly tripped while parading in front of her amused hosts.

Wedding bells for Prince Andrew and Fergie

Below: Prince Charles held a pre-wedding dinner for close members of the family, prior to Prince Andrew's marriage to Sarah Ferguson on 23rd July. Sarah and Diana famously dressed up as policewomen and tried to gatecrash Andrew's stag night at Annabel's night club.

Left: On a wet day in May, a suitably prepared Diana visited the Agricultural Show in Ipswich.

Opposite: Greetings for the elegant Princess as she arrived for a charity luncheon in aid of Save the Baby.

Diana at the ballet

Above: In her role as Patron of the British Deaf Association, Diana arrived at the Royal Opera House for a performance of *Ivan the Terrible* by the Bolshoi Ballet.

Opposite: Applauding the stars at the *London Standard* Ballet Awards, held at the London Coliseum.

Towards the end of a busy year, the Prince and Princess toured the Arabian Gulf. Diana was invited to King Fahd's palace in Saudi Arabia but was not allowed to dine with the men. The Sultan of Oman was very generous with his gifts, giving Diana priceless jewels and Charles an Aston Martin.

Getting into the spirit

Opposite above: As Charles and Diana toured Pinewood Studios to see the making of the new James Bond film *The Living Daylights*, the Princess had the opportunity to break a prop bottle over Charles's head!

Opposite below right: The Prince and Princess attended a glamorous ball at the Grosvenor House hotel to help raise a six-figure contribution towards the cost of Britain's challenge for the America's Cup. At the time, Prince Charles was Commodore of the Royal Thames Yacht Club, which was responsible for organising the attempt.

Opposite below left: In a variation on the same dress worn at the Grosvenor House hotel ball, Diana attended a screening of *The Mission* for the charity Birthright, at the Empire, Leicester Square.

Above: Diana was asked to open a new gallery at the National Maritime Museum in Greenwich, called 'Discovery and Sea Power 1450-1700'.

Christmas carols

Opposite: Accompanied by the Archbishop of Canterbury, Dr. Robert Runcie, Diana walked to the Carol Service at Canterbury Cathedral.

Above: Diana, after dropping William at Miss Mynors' kindergarten (left), and (right) in a different outfit she returned later that same day to attend the annual nativity play, in which William played the innkeeper.

1987

Against the elements

Opposite: On a windy day in January, Diana left the Help the Aged headquarters in Clerkenwell. Prince William had just started his pre-prep education at Wetherby School in Notting Hill, just five minutes from Kensington Palace. William was to settle in happily. His start at Wetherby coincided with a change of nanny, with Ruth Wallace taking over the role.

Left: The following week Diana opened a new unit at the Whitefield School for Deaf Children in Walthamstow, London.

Above: The Princess again set a trend when she attended a concert given by the London Philharmonic at the Royal Festival Hall, accompanying children from the London Borough of Tower Hamlets. The black and gold tassels on her stockings were soon noticed and copied.

Rumours about Charles and Diana's marriage were starting to increase as they attended more and more functions separately. Sharp-eyed members of the media noticed the tension between them and the absence of the warmth and devotion that they had once shared.

Musicals and ballet

Opposite: The Princess sported fashionable leather trousers for a performance of *The Phantom of the Opera* at Her Majesty's Theatre.

Above left: A bright pink bow tie dressed up her suit when she went to the London Hippodrome to see the jazz ballet *Nightcreature*.

Above right: In March, Diana again met Jimmy Savile at Stoke Mandeville Hospital, where she opened a new body scanner unit.

Right: Lionel Richie presented her with leather bomber jackets for the princes, decorated with their names. She was at the Lionel Richie concert at Wembley Arena in support of the British Institute of Florence and the Prince's Trust.

World Health Day

Opposite: World Health Day in April was marked by a Rubella Council luncheon at Marlborough House.

Above: Tree-planting duty at Sovereign's Parade, Sandhurst. Diana's military-style suit had been designed by Catherine Walker.

On a tour of Spain in April, they were guests of King Juan Carlos and his wife, Queen Sofia. At the end of the tour, Diana flew home alone, while Charles had a brief holiday in Italy.

Happy birthday to you!

Left and below left: Diana celebrated her twenty-sixth birthday at Wimbledon, where she watched a riveting match on the centre court between Lendl and Leconte. She was given a rousing chorus of 'Happy Birthday' by fellow spectators. Watching with her were Princess Michael of Kent and Mrs Catherine Soames, a close friend with whom Diana played tennis regularly. The Princess attended Wimbledon as often as she could and was always an enthusiastic supporter.

Opposite: Diana with Harrods boss Mohamed Al Fayed. He was a close friend of Earl Spencer and Diana had known him since she was eight. They watched as Charles scored four goals when his Windsor Park polo team beat the Guards. The match was organised by Al Fayed and they were playing for the Harrods Trophy. £30,000 was also raised for the Malcolm Sargent Cancer Fund for Children. Al Fayed then laid on a tea party for fifty children suffering from cancer, many of whom had a very short time to live. The children were overjoyed to meet the Prince and Princess of Wales *(opposite below)* but it was a very emotional occasion for all involved.

The new Bond movie

Having visited Pinewood Studios during the making of the film, the Prince and Princess attended the premiere of *The Living Daylights* at the Odeon, Leicester Square. Diana met the new James Bond, Timothy Dalton *(opposite below)* and his leading lady, Maryam d'Abo. It was during 1987 that Diana became determined to direct her energies towards a more fulfilling cause. She was a devoted mother and supportive wife, but wanted to use her compassion and caring nature to make a difference to other people's lives. During the year she realised that the Aids charities needed help and visited the first clinic at the Middlesex Hospital, meeting nine men dying of Aids-related illnesses, publicly shaking hands with a patient. Overnight she highlighted the help they needed and began to dispel the myths that surrounded the virus.

Meeting the former Beatles

Opposite: After the Prince's Trust Concert at Wembley in June, Diana was introduced to former Beatles George Harrison and Ringo Starr.

Above left: A stunning princess arrived at Charleston Manor in Sussex for a function in aid of the London City Ballet and the Purcell School.

Above right: Diana joined several other members of the Royal Family to greet the King of Monaco at a formal reception at Claridge's.

Freeman of the City

On 22nd July, Diana addressed four hundred guests at the Guildhall. She had just been made a
Freeman of the City and was noticeably nervous before she began to speak. First she had to
swear an oath of allegiance to the Queen, before making her own brief speech.

Support from the Spencer family

Above: As Diana spoke in response to being made a Freeman of the City, she was watched by *(left to right)*: the Lady Mayoress of London; Prince Charles; Lady Raine Spencer; her father, Lord Spencer; her brother, Charles Spencer, Viscount Althorp; her mother, Mrs Frances Shand Kydd and her grandmother Ruth, Lady Fermoy. Afterwards she made another speech at a lunch held at the Mansion House.

Opposite: A quieter day for Diana at Ascot Races. In August, she and Charles were once again guests of the King and Queen of Spain, this time for a family holiday at the Spanish Royal Family's villa in Majorca. After the holiday Prince Harry followed in his brother's footsteps and started at Miss Mynors' kindergarten in Notting Hill. He began at the school the day after his third birthday.

1988

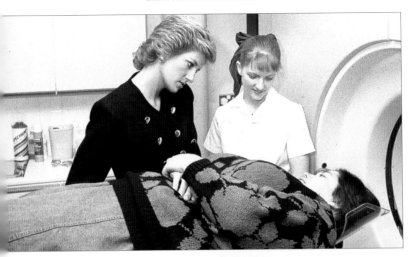

Patron of the ballet

Opposite: As patron of the London City
Ballet, Diana attended a charity performance
of the ballet *Talking Steps*. The evening was
organised to raise money towards a minibus
for the elderly.

Above: She was invited to open a new
x-ray department at the National Hospital for
Nervous Diseases. Compassionate as ever, in
the CT scanner room she made time to talk to
a patient and radiologists.

Right: A much shorter hairstyle and a purple
off-the-shoulder gown for the charity
premiere of *The Last Emperor*, nominated for
nine Oscars. The evening raised more than
£100,000 for the Prince's Trust.

The Prince and Princess toured Thailand in
February and the enthusiastic locals soon
christened her 'Thai Di'. She again flew home
alone while Charles went on safari with
friends in Tanzania.

Tragedy at Klosters

Above and left: In March, Major Hugh Lindsay, a great friend of Prince Charles, was killed in a skiing accident at Klosters. Prince Charles narrowly avoided being hurt as well. The Major's body was flown back to RAF Northolt in Middlesex and the coffin was carried from the plane by a guard of honour. Grim-faced, Princess Diana and the Duchess of York, also on the skiing holiday, attended the sad occasion.

Opposite: Zara Phillips and Prince William leave St. George's Chapel with Diana after the traditional Easter Sunday service

Sisters-in-law

Left: Sarah, Duchess of York, was expecting her firs baby when she joined Dian and other members of the Royal Family to welcome th King of Norway at Windso Castle, for a state visit.
Opposite: Diana chose an immaculately tailored dinner suit for a fund-raising greyhound meeting at Wembley - which only served to emphasise her femininity.

Wet Wet Wet!

Left: After a rock concert for the Prince's Trust at the Royal Albert Hall, two members of the band Wet Wet Wet were introduced to the Princess.

Above: A warm smile from Diana at the opening of a drug rehabilitation centre in Andover, Hampshire.

Opposite: Strapless and sensational at the premiere of the film *Crocodile Dundee*.

Royal wedding

Above: In July, Princess
Alexandra's son James Ogilvy
married Julia Rawlinson at
the Church of St. Mary the
Virgin in Saffron Walden,
Essex. Diana arrived with
Princess Margaret.
Left: At the opening of the
Barbican Fitness Centre,
Diana met swimmer Duncan
Goodhew *(centre)* and dance
Wayne Sleep. After he had
tutored her for her debut
dance at Covent Garden,
Diana had remained good
friends with the ballet dance
Opposite: A radiant Princes
in sea faring mood.

'Auntie Diana'

Opposite: Sarah, Duchess of York gave birth to her first daughter, Beatrice, on 11th August at the Portland Hospital, London. Diana was one of her first visitors, along with Princes William and Harry.
Above: Diana surrounded by well-wishers at St. Catherine's Hospice in Crawley, Surrey.

Working with Aids charities

Left: Newspaper proprietor Robert Maxwell greeted Diana as she arrived at the Guildhall for the launch of the National Aids Trust.

Above: Boxer Frank Bruno had Diana in stitches when she attended a London reception held by the British Sports Association for the disabled in aid of the disabled competitors and officials who would be travelling to the Paralympics in Seoul, South Korea. Afterwards he commented, 'She's a very beautiful lady'.

Opposite: Another favourite dress is given a second outing at the Annual National Service for Seafarers at St. Paul's Cathedral, London.

Patron of the Child Accident Prevention Trust

Opposite and right: In October, Diana attended the Annual General Meeting of the Child Accident Prevention Trust. At the meeting she raised the issue of dangerous toys and asked everyone buying children Christmas gifts to ensure the toys were totally safe.

Below: The Annual General Meeting of one of her favourite charities, Barnado's. As President, Diana had recently been filmed visiting a family fostering three children in Tottenham. The five-minute clip was part of a documentary showing people how under-privileged children could be helped in the right environment. Diana had stayed to talk to the family long after the filming had finished.

Drug-busting

Above and opposite above: In the Isle of Wight, she named a new customs boat at Cowes. *The Vigilant* was the first of a new breed of cutters that could use high speed and advanced radar and communications equipment to intercept drug smugglers.

Opposite below: In warmer conditions, Diana was at a royal premiere at the Empire, Leicester Square. Afterwards, she met actor Warwick Davis.

In November, six hundred guests helped Prince Charles to celebrate his fortieth birthday at Buckingham Palace. The glittering, black-tie party went on until three in the morning but many friends noticed how distant Charles and Diana seemed. Similarly, on an official visit to Paris in the same month, there was little conversation between them.

hristmas at Sandringham

ining the Queen Mother and the members of the Royal Family at Sandringham Parish Church
: the Christmas Day Service.

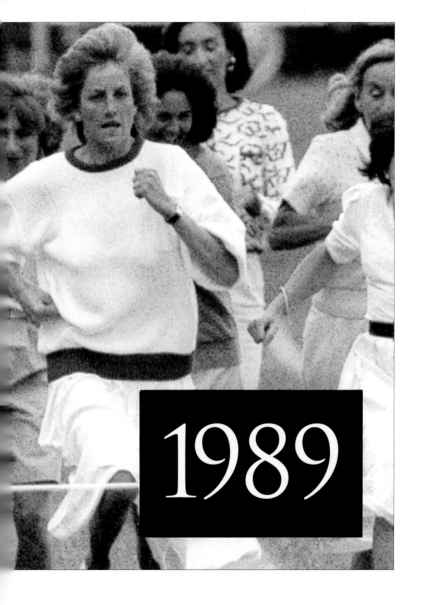

1989

Harry joins Wetherby School

Opposite: In January, Prince Harry followed William to Wetherby, his pre-prep school in Notting Hill. Teachers soon noticed Harry's natural academic ability and love of learning, which earned him a place in the top groups.

Above left: The Prince and Princess leave after the school run.

Left: Diana made a surprise visit to the Mayday Hospital in Thornton Heath to comfort survivors from the Purley rail crash. She met the driver of the train, who had broken both hips, and the youngest victim, aged four.

Above right: At the launch of the British Lung Foundation 'Bike 89'.

Crusade to end Aids prejudice

Opposite: Diana used every opportunity she could to counter the prejudice against Aids victims. During a visit to the Mildmay Mission Hospital in Bethnal Green, East London, she held hands with patients and sat down with them in the informal style that always endeared her to staff and patients. Earlier in the month she had cuddled a toddler in New York who was dying of an Aids-related illness, winning the hearts of the American people.

Right: In baseball hat and cowboy boots, Diana left Wetherby School after dropping Harry at the start of the summer term. Charles and Diana toured Kuwait and the United Arab Emirates in March, again departing separately when their official duties were over; Diana returning to England and Charles painting in Saudi Arabia.

Return to Riddlesworth Hall

Opposite: In April, Diana returned to her old school, Riddlesworth Hall in Norfolk. She was invited to open a new annexe, where pupil Stephen Keregari helped her unveil the commemorative plaque.

Above: Prince Harry rushes ahead to attend William's school concert at the Palace Theatre.

Flower festival

Right: Diana and Cardinal Basil Hume chatted happily at the Festival of Flowers Service in Westminster Abbey. Later she greeted the crowds outside the abbey. *(opposite below)* **Opposite above right:** The Princess arriving at the Savoy Hotel for the Floral Luncheon for Forces Workshops. **Opposite above left:** A wry look from Diana as she waited at Victoria Station with Prince Charles and other members of the Royal Family to welcome the President of Nigeria for state visit.

The eyes have it

People that met Diana were always struck by her expressive cornflower-blue eyes and the smile that lit up her whole face.

Colonel-in-chief

Above: As new colonel-in-chief to the 13th /18th Royal Hussars, Diana made her first visit to their barracks at Tidworth in Hampshire. The soldiers known as 'The Lilywhites' presented the Princess with a bouquet, and she watched an exhibition as ten men lifted each other on their shoulders to form a human triangle.

Left: Diana struggled with a fountain pen during a visit to the ante-natal clinic at the Queen Elizabeth II hospital in Welwyn Garden City, Hertfordshire.

Opposite: A warm June evening as Diana was escorted by David Lloyd at a celebrity night organised at his tennis centre in Raynes Park.

Sports day star!

Opposite above: After dispensing with her shoes, Diana cut a dashing figure as she managed a very creditable second place in the mothers' eighty-yard sprint at the annual Wetherby School Sports day.

Opposite below: At the Chalfont Centre for Epilepsy, Diana helped a resident to cut her ninety-sixth birthday cake.

Above: Four-and-a-half-year-old Prince Harry attending the Easter Sunday service at St. George's Chapel, Windsor Castle with his mother.

Viscount Althorp marries

Above: In September, Diana's brother Charles married Victoria Lockwood, a twenty-five-year-old model and the daughter of a civil aviation executive. The wedding took place on the Althorp Estate in Northamptonshire with Prince Harry as a pageboy. Diana arrived with William and Charles.

Opposite: Diana at the wedding with her mother, Mrs Frances Shand Kydd.

Motorfair

Opposite: On an unannounced private visit, Diana and Prince William rushed into the Motorfair at Earls Court. Their first stop was at the Ferrari stand to admire the new Testarossa priced at £107,000.

Right: Red was always one of Diana's favourite colours and she made a striking figure in this outfit on a visit to RAF Wittering.

Remembrance Day

Opposite and below right: A sombre moment as Diana, wearing a military-style outfit, in appropriate colours, laid a wreath at the Guards' Chapel in Wellington Barracks, London.

Left: As newly-appointed president of the Royal Academy of Dramatic Art, Diana installed Sir John Gielgud as the academy's first honorary fellow in recognition of his life's work.

Below left: Arriving for the Panasonic Sports Personality of the Year Award.

Lady in red

Above: Diana and Charles at 10 Downing Street, with Prime Minister Margaret Thatcher and her husband Denis.

Left and opposite: At the royal premiere of *When Harry Met Sally*, American stars Billy Crystal and Meg Ryan were introduced to the Princess. The premiere, held at the Odeon in Leicester Square, raised £50,000 for Turning Point, the charity, of which Diana was patron, aimed at rehabilitating alcoholics and drug users.

On the November tour of Hong Kong, locals this time called her 'Diana Wong Fei', which meant 'Diana, royal concubine'. While Diana flew home alone, Charles cruised around the South China Sea.

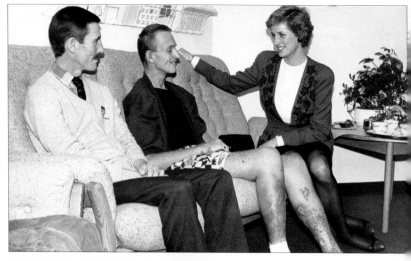

Further work with Aids charities

Above: After opening the Rodney Porter ward at St. Mary's Hospital in Paddington, Diana toured the hospital and was updated on its research programme. She then met patients and spent some time chatting to them. The new ward, financed jointly by the NHS and Aids charities, was to specialise in the treatment of Aids and carriers of the HIV virus. Diana had also made a very significant visit to Jakarta in November when she famously shook hands with people suffering from leprosy – once again she drove through all the myths and prejudice that could surround an illness.
Left: The annual walk to Sandringham Parish Church on Christmas Day.
Opposite: Unveiling a window at St Albans Abbey.

1990

Keeping fit with Fergie

Right: During the Duchess of York's second pregnancy, Sarah regularly swam with Diana. Sarah and Prince Andrew's first daughter, Beatrice, was now eighteen months old and Sarah was determined not to gain the weight that she had put on in her first pregnancy. While spending the traditional Christmas and New Year at Sandringham they used a club near King's Lynn. After Eugenie was born, Diana continued to help her friend exercise to shift any excess pounds. Diana eventually asked fitness instructor Carolan Brown to be her own personal instructor. She would go to Kensington Palace so Diana could embark on an exercise programme in greater privacy. One of the first points she addressed was Diana's posture. She was 5 feet 10 inches tall and, consequently, had a tendency to stoop.

Opposite: Appropriately attired for a visit to the Shia Islamic Centre in Stanmore.

Below: In February, she launched the centenary year of the British Deaf Association.

Concern for the homeless

Below: Diana always showed concern for the plight of the homeless and visited a Day Centre for young homeless people in Adelaide Street, London. She was also very keen to show her sons the different lives that some people were forced to lead and in 1993 organised a secret visit for the boys to a night shelter run by a group of nuns.

Opposite: Protective glasses were needed during a visit to BT & D Technologies Ltd in Ipswich.

Right: At the premiere of *Steel Magnolias*, Diana met (left to right): Sally Field, Olympia Dukakis, Daryl Hannah and Julia Roberts.

State visit to Nigeria

Above: Diana chose a dress in Nigeria's national colours for her arrival on a five-day visit, which began with a greeting by the president's wife, Madame Ankanobi. Prior to the visit the Prince and Princess of Wales had had anti-typhoid and yellow fever inoculations. They toured in temperatures of 110°F.

Opposite: Laughter at the Metropolitan Police Driving School, Hendon. Later that year, ironically, she would be on the wrong side of the law when she was caught speeding one morning in High Street Kensington. She went through a pelican crossing red light at seven in the morning.

'irgin Islands holiday

,pposite: A spring break was spent with the boys in the Virgin Islands.

,ove: A tanned Princess on return from the holiday met actor Sean Connery at the premiere of
,e Hunt for Red October.

Thoughtful Diana

opposite above and below: After officially opening the Depaul Trust housing for homeless youths project, Diana spoke to Cardinal Hume and one of the young people involved.

above: In temperatures that soared into the eighties, Diana made a visit to Lorne House, a hostel run by Turning Point, for those with drink and drug related problems. Instead of leaving as planned, she went to talk to a crowd in a nearby courtyard who had waited over an hour in the sweltering heat to see her.

Lunch with the Viscount

Opposite below left and right: She met her brother Charles, Viscount Althorp, for lunch at her favourite restaurant, San Lorenzo's. His wife, Victoria, was expecting their first baby at the end of the year.

Left and opposite above: The National Aids Trust organised a day conference on 'Women, Aids and the Future', at London's Commonwealth Institute.

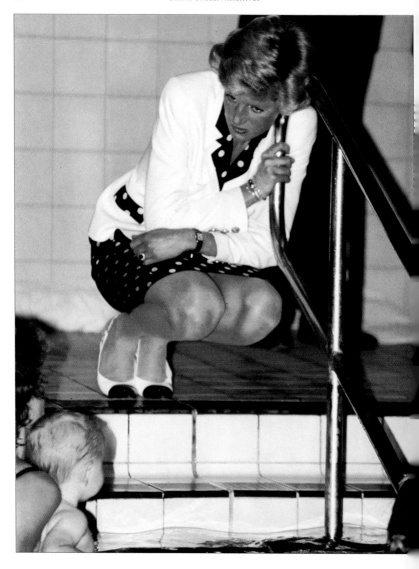

chool sports day

opposite: As part of her work to promote the Health and Fitness campaign 'Swimfit 90', .ana visited the Queen Mother Centre in London.

bove: At this year's Wetherby School sports day, Diana came third in the eighty metre others' race. Later in the day, she was seen to smack Prince William, as he ran away when e wanted to leave.

Charles breaks an arm

Left: In June, Prince Charles shattered his right arm in a polo accident. It was initially set at a hospital in Cirencester but he then had to go to the Queen's Medical Centre in Nottingham for further treatment. A titanium plate was attached to the bone and a piece of bone was taken from his hip to help heal the fracture.

Opposite above left: Resplendent in red and white for the Garter ceremony at Windsor Castle.

Opposite above right: A visit to Halliwick College, Winchmore Hill in North London, a residential college for students with disabilities.

Opposite below: Diana greets her sister-in-law, Sarah, at Wimbledon.

Using sign language

Opposite: At the British Deaf Association centenary congress, she made a faultless speech using sign language. The eight hundred delegates were delighted and gave her a standing ovation. She had been learning to sign for seven years in her role as patron to the association.

Left: Diana arrives at the English National Ballet at the Coliseum in London.

Charles convalesces

Below: William and Harry arrived at the Queen's Medical Centre to visit their father. He was due to return home the following week.

Left: A very pale-looking Prince Charles leaves the Queen's Medical Centre to travel by helicopter to convalesce at Highgrove. He was still limping and confessed to feeling 'awful'.

Above: Harry's sixth birthday treat was a surprise visit to the Battle of Britain 50th anniversary exhibition with a group of school friends. He had always been interested in the military and here he had the opportunity to sit in the cockpit of a Harrier jump jet and was shown how to operate a World War II Bofors anti-aircraft gun. The group then returned to Kensington Palace for tea.

In September, William began his prep school days at Ludgrove School in Berkshire. The boarding school was reasonably close to Highgrove and Kensington Palace, had a friendly atmosphere and a good sporting reputation. Most significantly it was set in 130 acres and was set well back from the road, which would give him maximum privacy.

We all have to shop sometime!

Above: A new Birthright booklet on healthy eating for pregnant women was published and Diana attended the launch at Tesco's in Southport.

Opposite above: A charity gala performance of Noel Coward's *Private Lives* at the Aldwych raised £100,000 for the Royal Marsden Hospital's Cancer Appeal. Joan Collins played one of the lead roles.

Opposite below: During a day's visit to Portsmouth, Diana played with a rabbit at the Portsea Adventure Playground.

In October, she made a solo visit on Concorde to Washington DC. There for twenty-two hours she visited Grandma's House, a home looking after children with Aids, in a very deprived area. She picked up a three-year-old girl, dying of an Aids-related illness, who asked for a ride in her car. Diana and her detectives were near to tears after they had given her the treat she so desperately wanted.

Harry's first official function

Opposite: In October 1990, Harry joined his mother and brother for his first official function. He attended a memorial service at St. Paul's Cathedral for the 1,002 fire fighters who died in the Blitz.

Left: The London Palladium was the venue for a charity gala in October. The celebrity show was held in honour of seven-year-old Lerona Gelb who had been paralysed in a road accident. The show raised £100,000 fo the International Spinal Research Trust of which the Princess was patron.

Gulf crisis

Opposite: In November she visited the Gulf Crisis Emergency Unit at the Foreign Office. In the same month she and Charles returned to Japan for the enthronement of Emperor Akihito.

Above left: In Colchester Diana met Lady Amanda Ellingworth, Trustee of the Guinness Trust.

Above right: On a scheduled visit to Oxford, Diana decided to take an Intercity train from Paddington, accompanied by her bodyguard and lady-in-waiting. After a last minute dash for the train, she too had to endure delays caused by signal failure.

Right: She chose the red check suit again to open 'Orangerie Italiana 1990', an Italian fine arts and antiques fair, at Accademia Italiana in Rutland Gate, London.

Charity gala performances

Left: The London Symphony Orchestra concert at the Barbican was in aid of the Prince's Trust and Birthright.
Opposite: Glamorous in green, the Princess made a sparkling entrance when she arrived at the The Royal Lancaster Hotel six days later, in early December.

Good wishes for the troops

Opposite: As Diana inspected the graduates at Sandhurst, she sent a message of hope and encouragement to Britain's armed forces.
She recognised that many of the cadets would be going straight out to join their regiments in the Gulf.
Above: The premiere of *Hobson's Choice*.

1991

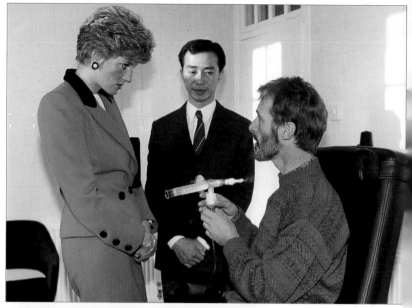

Compassion and care

Above: During a visit to the FACTS Health co-ordination centre in Crouch End, North London, Diana used every opportunity to talk to patients.
Opposite: At the Children of Eden gala performance at the Prince Edward Theatre, she took time to speak to twelve-year-old Claire Cowdrey.
Left: On tour in Peterborough.

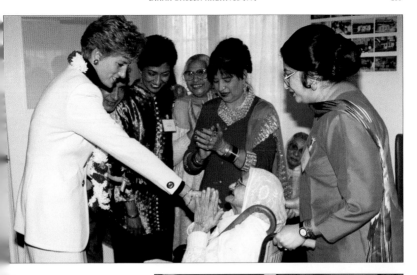

Day out at Alton Towers

Opposite: Diana loved taking William and Harry to 'ordinary' places so they could enjoy days out like any other family. Accompanied only by bodyguards, they queued up for rides and she insisted that they were given no special privileges. The boys had a wonderful time.

Above: In her capacity as patron of Help the Aged, Diana visited three hundred old people at an Asian Centre in Southall.

Right: The unveiling of the commemorative plaque when Diana opened the Oxford and Bedford Houses at Broadmoor Hospital.

Easter visits

Left: The royal premiere of *LA Story* was held at the Canon cinema in Shaftesbury Avenue.
Opposite above: During a visit to Great Ormond Street Hospital, the Princess stopped to talk to the mother of David Meaney, a three-year-old boy suffering from brain damage. During the conversation Diana quietly stroked the boy's hand and he woke for a moment.
Opposite below: At Windsor, with the Royal Family, for the Easter Service.

The school run

Opposite: Whenever possible, Diana would try to drop the boys at school herself. On this chilly morning, she had just taken William to Wetherby School after the Easter break.
Above: A dinner was held at the Mansion House to mark the launch of the Re Action Trust, a charitable venture between industry and Help the Aged. During her speech, Diana urged people to consider how much older people can still contribute to society.

Royal visit to Brazil

Left: During the visit, Diana took advantage of the hotel pool to have a very brief morning dip.
Below and opposite: Matching outfits for the Prince and Princess. They still maintained a happy image of their marriage when at official functions.

Helping others at home and abroad

Opposite: The Simple Truth charity concert at Wembley Arena raised £10 million to help the Kurdish refugees. Within hours of the concert finishing, money was to be sent to northern Iraq and would be closely followed by food, blankets and medical supplies. The money raised was to be matched by £10 million pledged by the government. Diana arrived at Wembley to support the cause.

Right and below: During a visit to open a new day hospital and family health clinic at Marlow Community Hospital in Buckinghamshire, the Princess went on a walkabout outside to meet the waiting crowds. When one elderly gentleman collapsed, she made her way through the crowds to kneel down and comfort him until the ambulance arrived.

Royal curtsey

Right: Protocol demanded that she curtsey to the Queen at a Mansion House function. In June, William, while at school, was accidentally hit with a golf club by a friend, knocking him unconscious. With blood pouring from the wound, he was rushed to the Royal Berkshire Hospital. His parents disagreed over which hospital should treat him but in the end Diana had her wish and he was sent to Great Ormond Street Hospital for Sick Children under police escort. He had a depressed fracture of the skull and needed a seventy-five-minute operation to assess the damage that had been caused. Diana stayed with him while Charles had to continue with his royal duties. William eventually made a full recovery.

Opposite above: Diana met Elton John during a charity performance of *Tango Argentino* at the Aldwych Theatre. Proceeds went to the National Aids Trust.

Opposite below: With Harry now at Wetherby, it was soon time for Diana to enter the annual mothers' race once again.

Thirtieth birthday

Opposite: In early July, the Prince and Princess were at the Royal Albert Hall for a gala performance of Verdi's *Requiem* by the London Symphony Chorus. It had been the Princess's thirtieth birthday a week earlier and press reports claimed that Charles had offered to throw a party for her at Highgrove but that she had declined. On the day she attended a lunch party at the Savoy in aid of the Rainbow House children's hospice appeal.

Above: Always a keen tennis fan, Diana was at Wimbledon.

Summer holidays over

Opposite above: After the annual summer break at Balmoral, Diana and the boys flew back with Prince Andrew and his daughters. There was time for a quick peck before the two families left in separate cars.

Above: After the premiere of *Backdraft* at the Empire, Leicester Square, introductions were made to Kurt Russell and William Baldwin.

Left: As colonel-in-chief of the Royal Hampshire regiment, she attended the regimental parade.

Opposite below: A gentle touch for one of the patients at the Royal Hospital and Home, Putney. The centre treated severely disabled people.

Celebration and tears

Opposite: His Aunt Sarah and cousins, Eugenie and Beatrice, joined in Harry's seventh birthday celebrations. A special birthday surprise was laid on in the grounds of Kensington Palace, which included a display by the police dog-handling team. Other people in the park watched as Harry whooped with delight at the sight of the dog-handler team clowning around with a display of cops and robber chases in which the dogs broke up fights between policemen wielding baseball bats.

Right below: In October, Diana was on an official engagement in the Midlands, when news reached her that five-year-old Leonora Knatchbull had died after a fourteen-month fight against cancer. She was the great-granddaughter of Lord Mountbatten and her parents, Lord and Lady Romsey, were very close friends of the Prince and Princess of Wales. Only a few days earlier, Diana had spent several hours at the hospital with Leonora.

Right above: In September, Diana made a solo four-day tour of Pakistan. She visited a Family Welfare Centre in a small village just outside Islamabad, receiving a traditional garland when she arrived.

Canadian tour

Left: In October, the whole family were involved in the official tour of Canada. The boys flew out the day before their parents, for security reasons. The tour marked the start of William's grooming for his future role and he was to accompany his parents on some occasions, in an official capacity.
Below: One of the Princess's favourite photographs, which she kept in her dressing room in Kensington Palace. She had just flown into Toronto and had to endure a marathon reception before she could see her children. She rushed across the deck of the Royal Yacht *Britannia* and threw her arms round them.
Opposite: Aboard a helicopter as it flew over Niagara Falls.

Further work with the National Aids Trust

Opposite above and below: At a conference organised by the National Aids Trust, Diana listened to teenagers' views on ways to improve sex education, to help protect young people from contracting the HIV virus. She listened carefully to their ideas, often making notes, and met them more informally afterwards.
Above: At Milestone House, Diana had tea with a lady suffering from Aids.

Dance for Life

The Dance for Life event at Her Majesty's Theatre marked World Aids Day. The evening featured the Royal Ballet and dancers from *Cats* and *Phantom of the Opera*, raising £150,000 for Crusaid. It was only three months since Diana's close friend Adrian Ward-Jackson, Governor of the Royal Ballet, had died of an Aids-related illness.

Opposite: When presenting the Princess with flowers, four-year-old Nicola Gerry asked Diana for a kiss.

Above: Meeting ballet dancer Darcey Bussell, after the show.

Right: Seven-year-old Harry holds his mother's hand on the way to Sandringham on Christmas Day.

In 1991, *Hello!* magazine voted her 'the most elegant and stylish woman of the year'.

1992

Day trips

Opposite above: Keen to let her sons lead as normal a life as possible, Diana would often use the local shops in Kensington High Street. No surprise then, when she was spotted queuing up for a McDonald's, one Sunday afternoon in January!

Opposite below: At Cardiff Arms Park, she and the boys watched as Wales lost 9-12 to France in the Five Nations Championship. She sang lustily with the rest of the crowd but the boys weren't quite so vocal!

Right: At the Taj Mahal, on a visit to India, Diana spent several minutes in solitude.

The Taj had been erected by Moghul Emperor Shah Jahan, as a memorial to his wife, who died in childbirth. This was the photograph, published around the world, that seemed to confirm Diana's loneliness and unhappiness in her marriage.

Tour of India

Opposite: In a very moving visit, Diana met many disabled 'untouchables', also known as 'God's People', who were from the lowest Indian castes. They gave her the traditional sign of respect by reaching for her ankles and she immediately moved closer and spoke to them through an interpreter. She met them at a welfare centre where residents were supported by British donors in an 'adopt a granny' scheme. It was run by Help the Aged - the Princess being a patron - who were supporting 6,000 elderly people in India at the time. After Charles had left at the end of the tour, Diana visited Mother Teresa's hospice in Calcutta, meeting every patient who was near to death.

Right: The Prince and Princess during the tour.

Below: When Diana presented medals after a polo match, the 20,000 strong crowd watched as Prince Charles moved to kiss his wife. However, Diana deliberately turned at the last moment to avoid his embrace.

Meeting Mother Teresa

Above and left: Soon after the India tour, Diana travelled to Rome where she had the opportunity to meet Mother Teresa.
Opposite above left: The royal premiere of *Hear My Song* raised £75,000 for Turning Point. The Princess addressed the audience asking them to try to understand the plight of the mentally ill. During the evening, Josef Locke, on whose life the film was based, became one of Michael Aspel's victims for *This Is Your Life*. The Princess had known about the plan and delightedly joined in with the applause.
Opposite above right: In her role as President of Barnardo's, she made a visit to the St. Luke's Day Care Centre in Deptford.
Opposite: A visit to the Institute of Child Health.

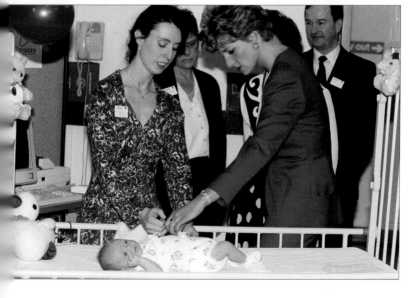

The death of Earl Spencer

Above and left: In March, Diana's father, Earl Spencer, died from a heart attack at the age of sixty-eight Diana adored her father, who had passed away while she was on a skii holiday. The funeral at the church c St. Mary the Virgin, near the Althor Estate in Northamptonshire, included many joyful hymns at the Earl's express wish. Diana's message of farewell on a wreath of lilies, swe peas, stocks and freesias said simply 'I will miss you dreadfully, darling daddy, but will love you forever. Love Diana.' The service helped to reunite the Earl's three daughters with their stepmother, Raine.

ove: In May, friends and family gathered at St. Margaret's Westminster to pay tribute to the
Earl Spencer, in a moving memorial service. The Rev. Dr Donald Grey, Canon of
stminster, led the service. He summed up the Earl as 'a loyal husband, a loving father and a
quely wonderful grandparent'. Bank of England Governor Robin Leigh-Pemberton, who had
wn the Earl since their schooldays, gave the address.

olo tour of Egypt

1 a solo trip to Egypt, Diana visited the pyramids. Apparently, photographers were very
appointed with the colour of her outfit, as it blended into the background.
posite above: Britain's leading acappella group 'Black Voices' was invited to perform at St.
phen Walbrook, a church in the City of London. Diana thoroughly enjoyed the performance
1 met the singers afterwards.
posite below: With her boys, after the Easter Service at Windsor.

Distress at drug addiction

Above: Diana was asked to make a keynote speech at a Turning Point conference. However, afte
watching the premiere of a ten-minute film on drug addiction, she was visibly distressed and
needed time to compose herself before speaking to the audience.

Opposite above and below: The Prince and Princess arrived separately for the Garter
Ceremony at Windsor Castle when Sir Edward Heath, Viscount Ridley and Baron Sainsbury
were installed as Knights of the Garter. Although they smiled and waved to the crowds there w
very little communication between them.

In June, the Andrew Morton book, *Diana, Her True Story* was published, which claimed to tell
the truth about Diana's unhappiness. He had used material from interviews with Diana's
friends. There was much speculation about Diana's involvement in the content and detail of th
book. After this, Charles and Diana were barely on speaking terms.

Visits around Britain

Opposite above: A visit to the Erskine Hospital for Disabled Servicemen in Glasgow.

Opposite below: Despite the obvious security risks, the Princess delighted the people of Belfast by visiting the newly restored Church House headquarters of the Presbyterian Church in Ireland and later attended a garden party at Hillsborough Castle.

Right: A bouquet from two-year-old Jade Symons at the Royal Albert Hall.

Below: With the children at a Barnardo's conference.

The Proms

Above: Crowds gather to welcome Diana to the First Night of the Proms at the Royal Albert Hall.
Opposite: A perfectly co-ordinated Princess at the opening night of the Australian ballet at the London Coliseum.

Greek island tour

Above: In August, Charles and Diana took their sons to Greece to begin a cruise in the Ionian Sea. They boarded a luxury cruise ship, the *Alexander*, lent to them by family friend and oil tycoon, John Latsis. The ship was equipped with three speedboats, an eight-seater helicopter and a chandeliered ballroom. The holiday was widely seen to be a last attempt to repair their ailing marriage.

Opposite above: At the First Night of the Proms she was greeted by Prime Minister John Major.

Opposite below: Meeting a patient at the London Lighthouse hospice.

'Just Like A Woman'

Left: Diana dazzled the crowds when she arrived for the royal charity premiere of *Just Like A Woman*. The evening raised vital funds for leukaemia research and she later met the film's star, Julie Walters, whose daughter Maisie suffered from the illness.
Opposite: The Prince and Princess arrived together for the commemoration service marking the 50th anniversary of the battle of El Alamein.

Half-term treat

Above: At Earls Court for the Queen's 40th Anniversary Gala.

Left: For an October half-term treat, Diana took the boys to Buckmore Park near Rochester in Kent. She had bought go-karts for them and they confidently raced the machines around the track at speeds of up to 50mph.

Opposite: The Princess won praise from Junior Health Minister Baroness Cumberledge who, at an Aids conference, credited Diana with having a significant influence on government policy.

Royal visit to
South Korea

Above left: On a four-day visit to
South Korea, Diana visited the Seoul
British School.
Above right: Honouring troops at th
Welsh Guards Memorial Service.
Left: Diana won the hearts of the
French during a two-day visit to Pari
She was away for Prince Charles's
forty-fourth birthday.
Opposite: At the International
Convention Centre in Birmingham,
she met some of the sponsors of
Turning Point and viewed a display
on Drugs Prevention Week.

A marriage in trouble

Opposite above: Diana was only too delighted to meet Paul and Linda McCartney when he performed his *Oratorio* at a concert hall in Lille.

Left: Addressing drug abuse specialists.

Above: The royal couple were clearly unhappy in each other's company.

Above: The Royal Variety Performance was the last joint engagement before their separation. On 9th December, it was announced in the House of Commons, by Prime Minister, John Major, that the Prince and Princess of Wales were to part. There was to be no question of divorce, and if Charles were to become King, she would become Queen. The previous week, they had both removed belongings from their respective homes - Charles would now officially be at Highgrove and Diana at Kensington Palace.

The marriage ends

Above: Diana meets Wayne Sleep again after a charity performance of *The Nutcracker* by the English National Ballet. The event, hosted by Foreign Secretary Douglas Hurd, raised money for English National Ballet and the Foundation for Conductive Education, which was aiming to build a national institution, mainly for the treatment of children suffering from cerebral palsy.

Left: Diana left Buckingham Palace, alone, after the announcement.

1993

High jinks at Thorpe Park

With only their nanny and personal detectives in tow, Diana took William and Harry to Thorpe Park, their favourite theme park. Dressed in jeans and sweatshirts, they queued up for rides and enjoyed the thrills, often getting soaked in spray!

The Jungle Book

Opposite above: Diana joined families all over Britain by taking her sons to see *The Jungle Book*. The twenty-six-year-old film had been re-released for the third time, with more than five million people buying tickets to net in excess of £4 million.

Opposite below left: In a very moving speech, Diana spoke to a large audience of health professionals at the Eating Disorders conference. She spoke of the despair and lack of self-esteem people endured and obviously drew on memories from her early childhood. Diana was believed to have suffered from bulimia during the early years of her marriage.

Opposite below right: A dinner for the British Wheelchair Sports Foundation at the Banqueting House, London.

Right: On walkabout in Oxford.

Below: Diana meets opera singer, Rebecca Evans.

Colonel-in-chief

Right: In June, Diana attended a military ceremony to take up the post of colonel-in-chief to the newly formed Princess of Wales's Royal Regiment. It had been created from a merger of the Queen's and the Royal Hampshires and troops had already been nicknamed 'Di's Guys'. She watched as a team of free-fall parachutists dropped from 3,000 feet to present her with a gold and diamond regimental brooch. During the ceremony, Diana addressed the troops, and to the delight of the crowd announced, 'It has to be said that for a thirty-one-year-old woman to have 2,500 men under her command is quite a feat, but I am sure I will rise to the occasion'!
Above: Supporting the Serpentine Gallery Renovation Appeal.
Opposite above and below: On walkabout in Cambridge town centre.

Tour of the sick and needy in Zimbabwe

Left: A visit to Zimbabwe soon became known as 'the suffering tour' as she met and comforted the sick, those dying from Aids-related illnesses and leprosy victims. She flew out to see the work being done by the major charities, who were delighted to involve her; Diana's presence was guaranteed to highlight any cause quickly and effectively. She was also highly respected for her genuine compassion and concern.
Above: Diana was greeted by the Brazilian ambassador, Senor Paulo-Tarso Flecha-Lima at Tiffany's in Bond Street, where she viewed the Schlumberger jewellery collection. His wife Lucia was a very close friend of Diana's giving the Princess a great deal of support when she needed it most.

bove: Diana spoke to children on a very successful tour of Nepal. She travelled with Lynda
Chalker, Minister for Overseas Development, visiting British Aid projects. During the year, it
became clear that Diana's official foreign trips would become more limited but she was
determined to continue the charity work that she knew was so effective. She therefore
approached charities such as the International Red Cross, who were delighted to work with her
in organising future foreign visits.

Death of Lady Ruth Fermoy

Opposite: The Prince and Princess were briefly reunited at the funeral of Diana's maternal grandmother, Lady Ruth Fermoy when they arrived together for the service at St. Margaret's Church in King's Lynn. They accompanied the Queen Mother, who had lost her oldest and closest friend and also her lady-in-waiting for three decades. Lady Fermoy had found her loyalties divided when Charles and Diana's marriage broke down but despite reports of a rift between Diana and her grandmother, they had spent a great deal of time together just before she died. After the internment at St. Mary Magdalen's Sandringham, the Prince and Princess left in separate helicopters.

Above left and right: At the Red Cross feeding station at Mazerera, Diana took on the role of feeding the children, some of whom had to walk ten miles a day to reach the centre. She dished out the meal of dhovi – a stew of ground peanuts, French beans, cooking oil and refined meal. The children were delighted when she gave out double the normal rations.

A separate Christmas

Right: On Christmas Day, Diana was resplendent in scarlet and black as she walked to church for the Christmas Day service. However, afterwards, she kissed William and Harry and spent Christmas elsewhere.

Opposite above: A relaxed and tanned Diana watching the performance at the Indiana Jones Adventure, Walt Disney World, Florida. She had taken the boys there in August.

Opposite below: As Diana performed her penultimate public engagement, she opened the St. Matthew's Community Centre at the Elephant and Castle in South London. Her hand was kissed by a royal fan!

On 3rd December, during a function at the Hilton Hotel, Diana decided to step down from public life. She stated that she needed 'time and space' after being the centre of media attention for twelve years.

1994

Reunion with Mother Teresa

Opposite: Diana met Mother Teresa at the Missionaries of Charity in Kilburn and the two greeted each other like old friends. Mother Teresa had flown into England en route from Washington to India, especially to see Diana. The two women had a great deal of respect for each other's work and Diana was invited to return to Calcutta to see the progress the mission had made on the streets.

Above right: At a family lunch at Scalini's, Diana met up with her brother, Earl Spencer, and her mother, Frances Shand Kydd. Charles Spencer's wife, Victoria, and their eldest daughter Kitty, aged three, accompanied them. They also had twin girls, Eliza and Amelia, aged seventeen months and Victoria was pregnant with their fourth child, due the following month.

Below right: Diana travelled from Paddington, with four friends, to watch the Wales v France international at Cardiff Arms Park. She clearly enjoyed herself amongst old friends, who produced a picnic lunch and bottles of Pouilly Fume!

Heir to the Althorp Estate

Opposite: Earl Spencer's wife, Victoria, gave birth to a boy, Louis Frederick in April. As their first son, he would inherit the title Viscount Althorp and the £90 million family estate. Diana arrived at St. Mary's, Paddington, to visit her new nephew. She came without any security protection and had to make her way through waiting photographers to get into the hospital.

Right: Diana joined William van Straubenzee, Catherine Soames and Kate Menzies for lunch at San Lorenzo's. Unable to park nearby, she had asked two Metropolitan Police officers to protect her car from traffic wardens, so they put official memos under the windscreen wipers.

Oops!

Opposite: Diana later found
out that the two officers had
been pulled up for their
actions and was fully intent
on apologising to them.
Right: Diana left Heathrow
Airport for her first official
engagement since retreating
from royal duties – she was
travelling to a Red Cross
meeting in Geneva.
Below: The Princess with
William and Harry at
Alton Towers. She had just
had her first sight of the
new 'Nemesis' ride and
ultimately declined to
go on it.

Camilla Parker Bowles

On 29th June, a documentary about Prince Charles, produced by Jonathan Dimbleby, was broadcast on television. During the interview, Charles admitted to adultery, after his marriage to Diana had broken down. The next day, Camilla Parker Bowles was named. He had had a relationship with her before she married her husband Andrew, and they had always remained very close friends. The night the programme went out to an audience of fourteen million, Diana attended a *Vanity Fair* party at the Serpentine Gallery. She wore a headline-grabbing black cocktail dress *(opposite)*.

Above and right: Diana arrived with Prince William to watch the women's final at Wimbledon. She sat with the Duchess of Kent.

Shopping in London

Diana had always enjoyed shopping in Kensington High Street close to her apartments at Kensington Palace. She could now move around more freely without having to be accompanied by protection officers.

Official visit to Paris

Right: In her capacity as President of Barnardo's, Diana made her first official overseas visit since she withdrew from public life the previous year. She had an informal lunch with President Valery Giscard d'Estaing and his wife, to foster links between Barnardo's and its French equivalent. From this moment onwards, she was to gradually resume more official and charity work.

Opposite: Guest of honour at a Versailles society ball in aid of a French children's charity.

Christmas

Above: Christmas Day with William and Harry.
Opposite above: Diana arrived at the Headway National Head Injuries Association fund-raising Christmas lunch.
Opposite below: Surrounded by admirers.

1995

Raising the alarm

Opposite: In January, Diana arrived at the Royal Parks Office in Hyde Park to present Royal Humane Society Awards to two men who had rescued a drowning tramp from a lake in Regent's Park. The Princess had been jogging in the park and had been the first person to raise the alarm. This was her first official engagement since the announcement of Camilla Parker Bowles's divorce at the beginning of the year.

Above: Diana took William and a school friend to Cardiff Arms Park to watch Ireland beat Wales 16-12.

Visit to Japan

***Opposite above and
below:*** On a visit to
Japan, she delighted her
hosts by speaking to
them briefly in Japanese,
one of the most difficult
languages to master. She
had been coached at
Kensington Palace for the
past year.

She then went on to give
a message of compassion
for the victims of the
Kobe earthquake. At the
Tokyo children's hospital,
one little girl thought she
was Cinderella.

Right: Diana at London
Fashion Week.

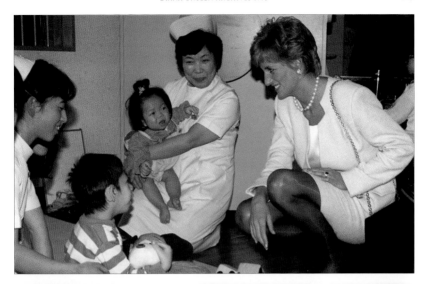

Di's Guys

Opposite: The Princess returned to Canterbury to inspect the Princess of Wales's Royal Regiment at Howe Barracks. She was there to hand over the new colours to the regiment and was wearing the brooch presented to her by the free-fall parachute team on her previous visit. **Above:** While there, Diana met World War I veteran Bill Pierce, who was one hundred and four years old.

Russia and Venice

It was now two-and-a-half years since Diana's separation from Prince Charles and her public appearances, such as trips to Moscow and Venice, were becoming rare. At thirty three, the figure of the world's most photographed woman was changing too. In recent months she had been pursuing a rigorous training schedule in the gym and there was now a new outline to her once slim shoulders.

Above: Diana was patron of a trust fund set up to improve facilities at the Tushinskaya Children's Hospital in Moscow. The hospital was struggling to care for more than a thousand children and while there she met nurses at the training school.

Right and opposite: Diana in Venice with one of her new friends Hong Kong-Chinese millionaire and fellow art lover David Tang.

Unsung work with the homeless

Left and opposite above: In June, Diana opened a hostel in Willesden, North London, run by the Depaul Trust. During the day, Cardinal Basil Hume paid tribute to Diana's work with the homeless; he revealed that she would often make private visits to hostels.

Opposite below: Choosing a Versace dress, the Princess met Tom Hanks at the premiere of *Apollo 13*.

In July, the family took part in their last official engagement together. They attended the 50th anniversary celebrations of VJ Day in London and had appeared to be very happy as they sat watching the parade.

Wild West

In the summer, Diana took William and Harry to America where they rode horses in Colorado and went white-water rafting in Utah. They spent some time on Goldie Hawn's ranch in Aspen.

Left: The Princess was delighted to see her favourite performer, Luciano Pavarotti, again when she flew into Italy.

Opposite: At a literary review lunch.

William's first day at Eton

Above: William successfully passed his Common Entrance Examination and arrived for his first day at Eton in September 1995. Despite the fact that his parents were in the midst of divorce proceedings the whole family arrived together. Diana had always wanted her boys to attend the school, following in the footsteps of the Spencer family.

Opposite: Diana was invited to Argentina by the ALPI medical charity. While there she met the Argentinian president, toured hospitals and met juveniles drawn into drink and drugs rings. During a lighter moment she watched the whales in Puerto Piramides. On 20th November, Diana took part in a *Panorama* interview with reporter Martin Bashir. The programme captured an audience of twenty-three million as Diana talked about her eating disorders and admitted to a relationship with James Hewitt, who had since let her down. She openly discussed her relationship with Charles, which could not work as 'there were three of us in this marriage'.

Humanitarian of the Year

In a glittering ceremony in New York, Diana shared the award of Humanitarian of the Year with General Colin Powell *(opposite below)*. The award, presented at New York's Hilton Hotel, marked her caring and compassionate achievements over the past fifteen years. She made her acceptance speech to guests who had paid £750 a head to attend.

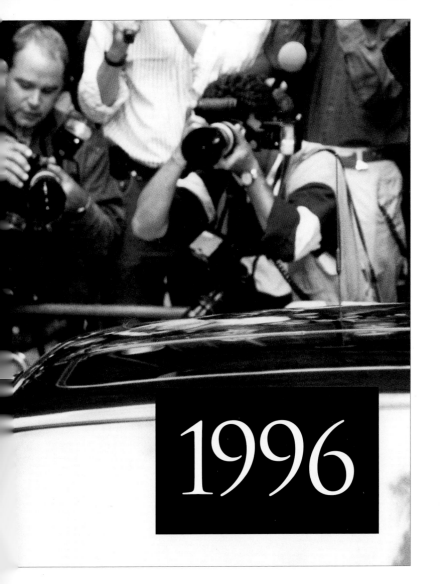

1996

Media attention

Opposite and right: Diana in
Kensington High Street. At
times she could shop almost
anonymously; at other times,
photographers would
surround her. She was now
able to move about without
an official protection team
and although it gave her more
freedom, it had its downsides;
she was often frustrated and
upset by the continual
attention of the media.

Below: On a visit to Italy, she
was surrounded by crowds as
she left 'Diana's Café'.

Decree absolute

Opposite above and below:
The divorce settlement was finally agreed between Charles and Diana, with the *decree nisi* announced on 15th July. Six weeks later when it was followed by the *decree absolute*, Diana fulfilled a previously planned commitment to visit the English National Ballet. She was still wearing her wedding and engagement rings. Charles was five hundred miles away at Balmoral, with William and Harry.

Above left: Diana took Chicago by storm when she arrived in June. Everywhere she went, crowds cheered and emotions ran high. One young boy reached out from the crowd to embrace her. She was there to raise money for breast cancer treatment, and attended the symposium on breast cancer at Northwestern University in Chicago.

Left: At a gala dinner in Chicago, she danced with American chat-show host Phil Donahue, amongst the dinosaurs at the Natural History Museum!

Divorce agreement

Under the terms of the divorce, Diana received a lump sum payment in the region of £17 million, but the title 'Her Royal Highness' was taken away. She decided to withdraw her support from a hundred charities, only maintaining involvement with six favourites: the National Aids Trust; the Leprosy Mission; Victor Adebowale's Centrepoint; the Royal Marsden NHS Trust; the English National Ballet; and the Great Ormond Street Hospital. She was trying to reduce her workload and concentrate on her future life as a single woman.

Opposite and above: Official functions in London.

Right: In October, Diana flew to Rimini.

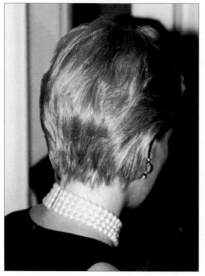

Humanitarian Award

In Rimini the Princess was presented with a humanitarian award for drawing the world's attention to the under-privileged.

Opposite above: Sitting with heart surgeon Christian Barnard at the award dinner. At the time, there was media speculation about a romance between Diana and heart surgeon Dr. Hasnat Khan. They were certainly very good friends and she had visited his family in Pakistan during the year, while she was there seeing her friend Jemima Khan.

Opposite below left: Sporting a new, sleeker hairstyle.

Opposite below right: At the end of the year Diana took Prince Harry, now aged twelve, to performance of *Riverdance*.

Above: With Mohamed Al Fayed for the launch of the *Heart of Britain* book at Harrods.

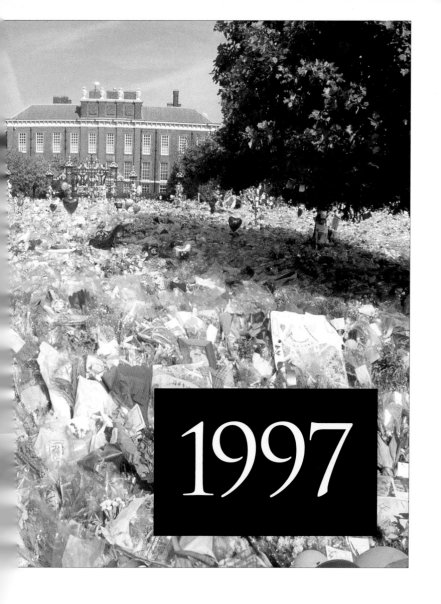

1997

Campaign against landmines

It was the Red Cross that first brought the landmine issue to Diana's attention. After attending a film premiere in aid of the charity, which was trying to instigate a world-wide ban on the weapon, Diana realised that this was another major issue where she could make a difference. A publicity visit to Angola was organised in January, with Diana travelling on behalf of the Red Cross.

The walk through a minefield

Diana was escorted by Mike Whitlam, director general of the charity in Britain. On arrival in Luanda they attended a mines awareness briefing session, where it was revealed that there was one amputee for every 384 inhabitants. She visited the most heavily mined areas and toured hospitals where she spoke to adults and children injured by stepping on mines. Shocked by what she had seen, she was determined to bring this issue to the world's attention. Working with the Halo Trust, the mine clearance team, she walked through the middle of a half-cleared minefield, knowing the global impact the photograph would have.

William's confirmation

Opposite: On departure from Angola.

Right: Prince William was confirmed in March 1997 at St. George's Chapel, Windsor. It was the first time that Charles and Diana had been seen together in public since their divorce the previous August. By this time, Charles and Diana's relationship had improved and they seemed more comfortable in each other's company. He would drop in to see her at Kensington Palace and they would attend the children's school events together.

Last hospital visits

Above: In April, Diana visited cystic fibrosis
sufferers at the Royal Brompton Hospital in
London.

In June, she flew to Washington to help
launch the American Red Cross anti-
landmines campaign. A gala evening held,
raised $650,000 for the charity. She flew to
New York to see Mother Teresa and attended a
breakfast meeting with Hillary Clinton. At the
end of the month, a charity sale of her dresses
was held. It was initially an idea of Prince
William's and eight hundred guests paid over
£100 each to attend the preview party. The
final sale raised over $3 million, with most of
the proceeds going to the Aids Crisis Trust.

Right and opposite: A new children's wing
was opened at Northwick Park Hospital on
21st July.

Continuing the campaign in Bosnia

In August, Diana flew out for a four-day visit to Bosnia, continuing to promote the Red Cross landmines campaign. She met landmine victims and bereaved relatives of those killed by the blasts, often reduced to tears by their plight.

Prior to the visit she had been holidaying with William and Harry in St. Tropez where they were the guests of Mohamed Al Fayed, on his luxury yacht. While there she met his son Dodi and there was much speculation in the media about a possible romance. On her return from Bosnia she spent some time with her friend Rosa Monckton, cruising around the Greek islands, before returning to France with Dodi on 21st August. She had left England for the last time.

Death of a Princess

On Saturday 30th August, Diana and Dodi were in
Paris and went to the Ritz for dinner. When they left,
they were besieged by the paparazzi and the Mercedes
in which they were travelling at high speed crashed in a
tunnel running parallel to the Seine. Dodi was killed
instantly, while Diana was cut free and rushed to a
Paris hospital. However, after two massive heart attacks
Diana could not be resuscitated and died in the early
hours of Sunday morning.

Her sons were at Balmoral with Prince Charles and he
had the daunting task of telling them the news when
they woke that morning. He then flew out to Paris to
escort her body back to England. People around the
world were stunned by the news and messages of
sympathy poured in. At Kensington Palace, the sea of
floral tributes grew by the minute and people queued
for hours to sign books of condolences.

Last farewell

Diana's funeral took place in Westminster Abbey on Saturday 6th September, with an estimated one million people pouring into London to line the procession route. In silence, they paid their last respects as the funeral cortège moved past, with her sons, Prince Charles, her brother Earl Spencer and Prince Philip keeping pace behind the coffin. After the dignified and moving service, thousands more lined the streets as the hearse took her body on its final journey to the Spencer estate at Althorp, where she was to be laid to rest on an island during a private family burial.

Diana, Princess of Wales, lost her life in the early hours of 31st August 1997, a month after her thirty-sixth birthday. That night she had enjoyed a quiet dinner at the Paris Ritz, with Dodi Fayed. The news of her untimely and tragic death shocked the world, with tributes pouring in from all continents. In London, people queued for twelve hours to sign the book of condolence at St. James's Palace and soon the sea of flowers that surrounded Kensington Palace was knee deep and growing bigger by the hour.

The country was devastated; for days the television channels replayed her life and the events that surrounded her death. The hearts of the nation went out to William and Harry, her 'beloved boys', then aged fifteen and twelve, and robbed of a mother they adored. The country stood still as her funeral took place the following Saturday, with a million people pouring into central London, to stand along the procession route. After a very moving and emotional service at Westminster Abbey, the crowds continued to mass along the route to Althorp where she was to be buried. In silent respect, the public lined the roads and bridges from London, throwing flowers onto the hearse.

Diana had won the hearts of the world when she married Prince Charles in a fairy-tale wedding at St. Paul's Cathedral in July 1981. Soon she was the mother of two sons, determined to bring them up with a mix of royal tradition and modern influences. Quickly established as a fashion icon and wife of the future heir to the throne, she was then determined to take on her own charity work and 'make a difference to people's lives'. She initially did this by cutting through all the misconceptions about HIV and Aids and walking into the Middlesex Hospital to shake hands with a patient. This was followed a few years later by a visit to a leprosy clinic where she sat on patients' beds and cuddled them, regardless of traditional fears of the disease.

Her charity work was phenomenal. She was patron to countless organisations and her concern was genuine. She was always happiest when she reached those who needed support, when she could talk to them and give reassurance: she left a huge and lasting impression on so many people's lives. In the few years before her death she took on the landmines issue, working closely with the Red Cross. In a matter of days she brought worldwide attention to the devastation that unexploded landmines were causing around the world.

Her marriage to Prince Charles gradually broke down in the eighties and they were finally divorced in August 1996. However, during this time their commitment to their sons was absolute. Royal tradition was often broken as they jointly made decisions about their schooling and social life. In William and Harry, Diana has left a fabulous legacy: they have both inherited many of the traits that endeared her to the British public. They have matured into men who are now ready to continue the work she started and will carry the candle of her memory.

Diana, Princess of Wales
1961-1997

Bibliography

Diana The Untold Story Richard Kay and Geoffrey Levy

Princess Ann Morrow

Diana Portrait of a Princess Jayne Fincher

Diana Story of a Princess Tim Clayton and Phil Craig

William The Rebel Prince Nicholas Davies

William The Inside Story of the Man Who Will Be King Nicholas Davies

Prince Harry The Biography Mark Saunders

Daily Mail and *Mail On Sunday*

Acknowledgements

The photographs in this book are from the archives of the *Daily Mail*.
Particular thanks to
Steve Torrington, Dave Sheppard, Brian Jackson,
Alan Pinnock, Richard Jones and all the staff.

Thanks also to
Cliff Salter, Richard Betts, Peter Wright, Trevor Bunting, Jane Hill,
Simon Taylor and John Dunne.